Oliver Joseph Burke

The South Isles of Aran

County Galway

Oliver Joseph Burke

The South Isles of Aran
County Galway

ISBN/EAN: 9783337407117

Printed in Europe, USA, Canada, Australia, Japan

Cover: Foto ©Andreas Hilbeck / pixelio.de

More available books at **www.hansebooks.com**

THE SOUTH ISLES OF ARAN

(COUNTY GALWAY)

BY

OLIVER J. BURKE, A.B., T.C.D.

Knight of the Order of St. Gregory the Great

BARRISTER-AT-LAW

AUTHOR OF "THE HISTORY OF ROSS ABBEY," "HISTORY OF THE LORD CHANCELLORS OF IRELAND," "HISTORY OF THE ARCHBISHOPS OF TUAM," "ANECDOTES OF THE CONNAUGHT CIRCUIT"

"Signs and tokens round us thicken,
Hearts throb high and pulses quicken"

LONDON
KEGAN PAUL, TRENCH & CO., 1, PATERNOSTER SQUARE
1887

(The rights of translation and of reproduction are reserved.)

TO

THE HON. MR. JUSTICE O'HAGAN,

ONE OF THE JUSTICES OF THE SUPREME COURT IN IRELAND.

———

MY DEAR JUDGE O'HAGAN,

During the vacation of last autumn I applied myself to collecting as much information as possible concerning the South Isles of Aran, which I had visited in connection with the Land Commission in the previous month of July. Pressure of business and a severe illness compelled me to defer until recently the arranging of my notes, which, in the hope that they may direct the attention of those in power to the long neglected Islands, I have resolved to publish, and I look on it as a good omen of the success of my efforts that you have kindly allowed me to dedicate my work to you, who have won so high a place in law and in literature.

        Believe me to remain

                Sincerely yours,

                      OLIVER J. BURKE.

OWER. HEADFORD.
  CO. GALWAY,
    August 8, 1887.

CONTENTS.

CHAPTER I.
PAGE

Island of Aran—Galway bay, anciently Lough Lurgan—Population—Religion, etc.—Inishmore, ruins on—Inishmaan, ruins on—Inisheer, ruins on—Mail boat—Hotel—Aran landscape—Flora—Potatoes—Aran wildfowl—Capture of the puffin—Cragsmen—Geology of islands—Limestone terraces—Boulders—Cliffs on islands—Seaweeds—Moving sands—*Pinus maritima* 1

CHAPTER II.

Monuments of Druidism—Druids—Cairns—Cromlechs—Baal, worship of—Zodiacal rings—Sacred fires—Druidical religion—Sir Edward Coke, on—Groves—Immense fortresses—Dun Ængus—Its situation, dimensions, etc.—Dun Conor—Christian remains—St. Enda, romantic story of—His hapless love—Becomes a monk—Obtains grant of Aran from King of Cashel—St. Brendon—His leaving Aran for countries beyond the Atlantic—Rendered into verse by Denis Florence MacCarthy—St. Columba, his grief at leaving Aran—Rendered into

viii   CONTENTS.

                                                                PAGE

verse by Sir Aubrey De Vere—St. Fursa—Residence in Aran—Pilgrimage to Rome—Buried in Aran—Aran monuments, pagan and Christian, vested in Board of Works—Churches facing the east—The north—Cloghauns—Dwellings of the monks—*Teampul-Chiarain*—*Teampul McDuach*—Holy well—Childless marriages—Description of churches—Lonely lives of the monks—One of the Popes said to be buried in Aran—Ordnance Survey—Its vast stores of learning unprinted 13

CHAPTER III.

Aran, 14th-18th centuries—A.D. 1308. O'Brien, lord of the isles—In consideration of twelve tuns of wine annually engages to protect the trade of Galway—A.D. 1334. Aran plundered by Darcy—A.D. 1400. Henry IV. gives license to certain persons to attack rebels in Aran—A.D. 1485. Franciscan monastery built—A.D. 1537. Suppression of religious houses—A.D. 1560. Shipwreck of Teige O'Brien, lord of the isles—A.D. 1570. Mortgage of the islands—A.D. 1579. Mayor of Galway appointed admiral of Galway bay, including Aran—1586. O'Brien expulsed from Aran by the O'Flaherties—1587. Queen Elizabeth grants islands to Sir John Rawson—1588. Corporation of Galway petition in favour of O'Briens—Annals, 1618, 1641, 1645, 1651—Surrender of the islands to the Commander-in-Chief of the Parliamentary forces—Annals, 1653, 1670, 1687, 1691, 1700, 1746, case of *Mayor of Galway v. Digby*—1754, 1786. Earldom of Aran—1857 31

CHAPTER IV.

Noble character of Aranite peasantry—Letters, 1841, by Dr. Petrie; 1852, by Sir Francis Head, K.C.B.; 1875, by Frank Thorpe Porter, Esq., B.L.; 1886, by Mr. R. F. Mullery, clerk of Galway Union; by Philip Lyster, Esq., R.M., B.L.—Rev. Fathers O'Donohoe, P.P., and Waters, C.C.—*Sta viator*—Isle of O'Brazil—Gerald Griffin's poem on 52

CHAPTER V.

Healthful islands—Old age in—Land Commission in Aran—Aran fisheries—Letters, 1886, from Sir Thomas F. Brady, fishery commissioner, on; from C. T. Redington, J.P., D.L., on public works in islands; from Rev. William Killride, on employment and on timber—"Many places in the islands covered with trees" fifty years ago—Poverty of fishermen—Baltimore fisheries—Baroness Burdett-Coutts—Irish Reproductive Loan Fund—Bounties given by Irish Parliament, in 1787, to encourage deep sea fisheries—Trawling 65

CHAPTER VI.

Re-afforesting Aran—Dr. Lyons—Dermot O'Conor Donelan, J.P.—Forest industries in Germany—Supports 300,000 families—Paper from young timber, etc. ... 82

CHAPTER VII.

PAGE

Superstitions of the grove—Concerning the oak—The ash—The mountain ash—The aspen—The pine—The holly—The ivy—The hawthorn—The blackthorn—The rose—The fern—The fairy flax—The hazel 88

APPENDIX A.

Conversant with the O'Briens—Bryan Boroimhe—His descendants Kings of Thomond—and their descendants Lords of Inchiquin, junior branch of Kings of Thomond—Marshal MacMahon—Also junior branch, O'Briens of Ballynalacken 105

APPENDIX B.

Statistics of Aran 110

THE SOUTH ISLES OF ARAN.

CHAPTER I.

> "Oh, Aranmore! loved Aranmore,
> How oft I dream of thee,
> And of those days when by thy shore
> I wandered young and free;
> Full many a path I've tried since then,
> Through pleasure's flowery maze,
> But ne'er could find the bliss again
> I felt in those sweet days."
>
> THOMAS MOORE.

THE south isles of Aran, which shelter the Galway bay from the heavy swell of the Atlantic, are Inishmore, the large island, nine miles in length; Inishmaan, the middle island, two and a half miles in length; Inisheer, the lesser, two miles in length; Straw Island, upon which the lighthouse stands, and the Brannock Rocks or islands, all forming that group which to the west bounds the Galway bay, and the ancient jurisdiction of the Admiral of Galway. They lie in a line drawn from the north-west to the south-east from Iar Connaught to the county of Clare. Iar Connaught is separated from Inishmore, the largest and most westerly island, by the North Sound, five and a half miles wide, called by the natives *Bealagh-a-Lurgan*, "Lough Lurgan way." Lough Lurgan was the ancient name of a lake that formerly lay west of Galway, and the tradition is that in the old times before us—213 years from the Flood—the waters of the Atlantic, sweeping in the full fury of their force across the Aran barriers, united with the waters of the lake and formed the Bay of Galway, leaving the islands of Aran the towering remnants of the barriers which were too strong even for the Atlantic billows to carry away. Between Inishmore and Inishmaan is Gregory's Sound, a mile and a half wide, called by the natives *Bealagh-ne-Hayte*, "Hayte's way." The present name was given to it by the monks, who called the sound "Gregory," in honour of Pope Gregory the Great, after he had converted or aided in converting the Anglo-Saxons to the Christian faith. Between the middle island, Inishmaan, and Inisheer, the eastern and smallest island, is the "foul sound," four miles wide; and between Inisheer and the county of Clare is the "south sound," four miles wide. This is the great waterway between "the old sea," as the natives call the Atlantic, and the Bay of Galway.

The sum of the lengths of the three islands and of the two intervening sounds is eighteen miles. The area of the entire group is 11,288 acres; poor law valuation, £1576; rent, £2067; poor rate, a shilling in the pound; average poor rate for ten years, three shillings; population, 3118 Catholics, and 45 Protestants. Aran is in the Catholic archdiocese and in the Protestant diocese of Tuam. In the islands are three Catholic churches and one Protestant, two priests, one parson, and one doctor, and there are schools, schoolmasters, schoolmistresses, and scholars, *et hoc genus omne;* and there is a petty sessions court, and there are three police-barracks and eighteen policemen. The fishing-boats or curraghs of the third class, which are ribs covered with canvas, and worth £6 each, are 130 in number; of the second class there are 34 boats, and of the first class there are none. There are no paupers from the islands in the workhouse, which is in Galway, and there is no workhouse on the island; neither is there an auxiliary workhouse, nor an hospital, nor an infirmary, nor a midwife, nor a jail, nor grand jury works, though there is a grand jury cess of £34 12s. 2d.

Of Inishmore, or the great island, Kilronan is the capital—a village with a good hotel. Killeany was the ancient capital, formerly the residence of the lords of the manor of Iar Connaught. The other places of note are Oghil, Onaght, Bungowla, Kilmurry, Dun Ængus, Dun Eochla, Dubh Chathair or the black fort. So also on that island are the ruins of the churches of Tempul Benin with its rectangular enclosures and group of cells, of Tempul Brecan and Cross, of Tempul Beg Mac Dara, of Tempul More Mac Dara, of Tempul Assurniadhe, of Tempul-an-cheathrair-Aluin, and of St. Enda and the ruins of the seven churches.

On the middle island of Inishmaan are the ruins of the fortresses of Dun Chona and Dunfarbagh, and the villages, five in number. On the eastern island of Inisheer are St. Gobnet's chapel, Ballyhees, Largi, Furmina, Trawkera, near which there is a lake a quarter of a mile in circumference and of great depth, which might be converted into a useful harbour by cutting an entrance into it through the rocky shore.

The harbour of Kilronan is spacious, but not fitted for vessels of heavy tonnage. A pier of four or five hundred yards is built out into the sea, alongside of which was moored during the tempestuous days of the last week of July (1886) her Majesty's mail-boat— a large-sized sailing yacht, provided with a cabin and forecastle, and manned by a remarkably civil and obliging crew. But it is to be lamented that no steamer has as yet been placed on the line between Galway and Aran, in consequence of which, frequently for four or five days, communication with the mainland becomes impossible. Letters remained unanswered, and newspapers remained unread; so that nation might rise against nation, and kingdom against kingdom, but the islanders in happy repose, undisturbed by the postman or by the magnetic wire, would in their isles of peace have happily lived on in blissful ignorance of the painful turmoils that reigned around.

At the hotel the tourist will be served with a homely and wholesome fare—prime veal and sweet and tender mutton, for the Aran herbage is renowned for the tenderness of the meat that it produces. At dinner a bottle of the mountain-dew, with a smell as divine as it is illegal, may be by accident produced; and for all this, when the guest requests that he might be informed of the charges, the reply ten to one will be, "Oh, anything your honour likes to give!"—at least, such was said by the black-eyed Hebè who ministered to the wants of the writer of these pages.

The Aran landscape as your vessel approaches from Galway is a peculiar one—peculiar to Aran. From the soft sea beach on the Galway side of the island, which varies in breadth from one to four miles across, slope fields of bare rocks terrace over terrace, sometimes nine in number, until they reach the topmost cliff on the south-west or ocean side hundreds of feet over the Atlantic. This terraced landscape has the appearance of being a barren and rocky wilderness; but on closer inspection threads of fresh green herbages can be traced in the cleavages and deeply cut fissures of the rocks, and it is in those cleavages that the richest profusion of botanical specimens are to be found. The cleft upon which we stood was teeming with purple heather, foxglove, scarlet geranium, and wild thyme, with the golden leaf of the variegated ivy; the crimson berries of the orchis and the red fruit of the wild strawberry forming a rich contrast to the delicate blue of the forget-me-not. Here, too, were the harebell and speedwell, fringed with the delicate frond of the maidenhair fern. In other clefts was the richness of the white and red clover, intermingled with a variety of medicinal herbs, amongst which were the wild garlic and the kenneen or fairy flax, much relied on for its medicinal qualities. In several of the localities in the islands the tormentil root, which serves in place of bark for tanning, and another plant which gives a fine blue dye and which the islanders use in colouring woollen cloths manufactured by them for their own wear, are to be found. The Aran isles contain many rare plants; but, owing to the absence of turf bogs and scarcity of damp ground, there are neither marshy nor heathy plants, nor sedges, nor rushes. Even so, the flora of Aran is decidedly rich. On the hillsides are a great variety of flowering plants indigenous to the soil, which blossom at different times of the year. In the rocky dells there are several kinds of convolvulus of very rich florescence. The Madagascar periwinkle seems to be perfectly acclimatized and blossoms profusely, and we were happy to find an abundant growth of hops, the introduction of which is ascribed to the monks of the olden time.

The tillage of the islands comprises potatoes, mangold wurzel, vetches, rape, clover, oats, and barley. The potatoes almost exclusively planted are "the Protestants;" and a Protestant tourist unarmed felt somewhat alarmed at the startling intelligence that "dinner would be ready as soon as the Protestants that were on the gridiron would be roasted." The dinner brought up, need it be told that our Anglican friend enjoyed the joke of our witty waitress quite as much as we ourselves did?

The crops are greatly devastated by caterpillars and grubs. The abundance of these pernicious insects is attributed to the great scarcity of sparrows and other small birds. Starlings are seldom seen; but never a swallow. Sea gulls are numerous, and amongst the sea birds the osprey or sea eagle is a conspicuous object. Neither the raven, rook, crow, nor jackdaw visits the islands; but there is a handsome bird which is very numerous, especially in the north island. The chough, which, in addition to plumage dark and glossy like that of the jackdaw, displays a beak and legs of bright scarlet. It is said that this bird was formerly to be seen in flocks on various parts of the English coasts, and that now it cannot be found in any part of the United Kingdom except in Aran. Plovers, gannets, pigeons, duck, teal, and divers breed abundantly on the rocky ledges. The cliffs are the resort of countless puffins (*Anas Leucopsis*); the popular belief being that they spring from the driftwood.* Their flesh supplies a rich lamp oil, and their feathers fetch a high price in the London markets. The capture of these birds is a dangerous occupation for the cragsmen, who descend from the cliffs by means of a rope to the haunts of the puffin, and having spent the night in the dangerous occupation, ensnaring and killing them as they sleep on the rocky ledges, they are hauled up in the morning, having realized ten or twelve shillings during the night. In the summer of 1816, two unfortunate fellows engaged in this frightful occupation missed their footing, and falling, were dashed to pieces on the rocks below. The solitary bittern, called in Irish the *Boonaun-Laynagh*, frequents the low-lying ground on the Galway side of the island, and hares and rabbits are very plentiful also. On the barren sheets of rocks the peasants (denominated lazy and idle, by lazy and idle writers and speakers) have with tireless toil walled in and made numberless gardens in which potatoes mealy and dry are grown. The meteorological aspirations of the Aran peasant are for rain, diametrically the opposite of what their brethren on the mainland desire. A dry summer gives to Aran a parched and burnt-up hue, when the cattle faint and die if not removed to the mainland. Tanks, such as they have in Ceylon, are sadly wanting

* Denis Florence McCarthy's Poems, p. 87 note.

in those islands, and the expense of their construction must be a trifling matter indeed.

One of the most remarkable features in the conformation of Inishmore is, that between the overlapping strata or terraces of limestone, thirty-seven feet in thickness in some places and eighteen in others, are beds of shale. The highest of the terraces is 320 feet over high-water mark, on the perpendicular cliff overlooking the Atlantic. On the sixth lowest of these descending steps the village of Kilronan, the capital of the island, over against the Galway bay, is built, and under that terrace and over the seventh is a shale bed which contains the water supply for the glebe and upper village wells.

Those who delight in geological speculations will find in these isles much to interest them. Here are deep furrows in the hard rocks, cut as they say by passing icebergs. One of these ice-cut furrows may be seen near the shore of Killeany Bay, about two hundred yards north-east of Lough Atalia, and a quarter of a mile from Kilronan. It is about seven yards long, nearly a yard wide, having a bearing of east by north. Though the icebergs have left their striæ, and though their passage is marked by the deep furrows cut by them as they moved, nevertheless the patches of boulder drift on the surface are few; but the bergs in their passage from the north district did drop some huge metamorphic rocks, not one of which is indigenous, so to speak, to the islands, but have been carried from a district such as that of Oughterard. Strange that some limestone boulders have also been dropped, carried from some far-off limestone district. These boulders have withstood the wreck of ages, but the weather-beaten rocks under them are so worn as here and there to present the appearance of pedestals bearing up the superincumbent masses. Whilst there is much to arrest the attention as you look from the hotel windows towards Galway over the Galway bay, bounded on the north by the grotesque desolation of the Connemara mountains, and on the south by the rocky mountains of the county of Clare, it is on the south-west side of the islands of Aran that the scene is awfully sublime, terrific, and impressive—rendered more awful by reason of the confusion of the waters and of the roaring of the waves of the sea. The heavy swell of the Atlantic there rolls in angry billows against the cliffs dark and perpendicular, hundreds of feet in height—cliffs perforated by winding caverns worn by the violence of the waves, from one of which, having an aperture in the surface, was projected a column of water to the height of a ship's mast. Whilst many of these cliffs rise perpendicularly from the ocean, many of them have sea terraces or steps at foot below the high-water mark. At *Illaun-a-naur*, on the south-easterly side of the great island, are sea-terraced cliffs which are fendered by a rampart formed of enormous blocks of limestone upheaved from the depths of the ocean and hurled with violence on the rampart which now forms a foot barrier against the further encroachment of the Atlantic.

The sea-weeds around the Aran islands are peculiarly fitted for the production and manufacture of kelp, of which there are two varieties, one made from the black weed, and the other from the red. The black usually grows above the low-water mark of the neap-tide, whilst all the red grows below it. The red weed kelp is the most valuable, as in general it gives salts containing iodine. Marine plants, such as the sea-anemones, the rock-grown samphire, and the sea-cabbage grow around the islands in great profusion.

Another remarkable feature in Aran is the enormous amount of fine quartzose—moving sands which, blown in thick clouds by the winds, fill the nooks and corners and crevices of the islands. These sands, which are said to possess the property of preserving bodies uncorrupted after death, might be fixed and utilized in the same manner as the sands of Arcachon on the west coast of France have been fixed and utilized, by planting therein vast forests of the *Pinus maritima*, the interlacery of whose roots would do the twofold duty of fixing the sands and creating a soil enriched by the amount of nitrogen therein digested and deposited. At Trawmore, on the south of Killeany Bay, proofs have lately been discovered not only of the movement of the sand-hills, but also of the appearance of fields and buildings submerged on the sea-coast. These islands in prehistoric times must have suffered much from the convulsions which then shook the world—in later times they appear to have suffered little, though Richard Kirwan the chemist relates that in his memory, in the year 1774, a fearful thunderstorm visited Inishmore, when a granite block of enormous dimensions, called the "Gregory," was struck by lightning, shattered to atoms, and flung into the sea.

CHAPTER II.

"Remnants of things that have passed away,
Fragments of stone reared by creatures of clay."
Siege of Corinth.

THE "remnants of things that have passed away" are many on these islands. In no other part of the United Kingdom are there confined in spaces so narrow so many monuments of Pagan times; here are evidences of two great ages of civilization—that of the Druids and that of the Christians; but, whether of the Druids or of the Christians, Aran had been the retreat in early times of the contemplative and the learned. Sequestered and undisturbed, the natives have even to this day preserved much of the moral and physical remains of the ancient world. The Aranites in their simplicity consider the remains of the Druids as inviolable, being as they fondly imagine the enchanted haunts and property of aerial beings, whose power of doing mischief they greatly dread and studiously propitiate. The natives believe that the "cairns" or circular mounds are the sepulchres of the mighty men of old, men of renown, whose acts and deeds even now are celebrated in songs sung at the cottage firesides by minstrels to the strings of the wandering harper: on every lip are the exploits of Churcullen, of Gol, son of Morna, of Oscar, and of Ossian, and here are pointed out the places where they lived and died. We have also the immense "cromlechs" or altar flags, supported on perpendicular pillars, as we may venture to call the unhammered stones of about three feet in height, whilst under those "cromlechs" still rest the remains of heroes whose faithful dogs interred with them bear them company even in death. Here, too, no bad memory is retained of the sacred fires of Bal (another name for the sun), which were kept burning; for the sun, and the moon, and the stars were by them reverenced; but the sun of the Druids was supposed to be the most noble type of the Godhead—the most glorious object of the material creation. The mysterious stones, twelve in number, encircling the altars of sacrifice, sometimes said to be zodiacal rings, after the twelve signs of the zodiac, are here frequently to be found. The purifying ordeals the cattle were subject to at Aran until a very late period are yet there remembered. The sacred fires on the first day of each of the quarters blazed from cairn to cairn, amid prayers for the fruits of the earth, and even yet, on St. John's Eve in June, huge bonfires are lighted near every village through the island, for the holy flame was considered essential to the cattle as a preservative from contagious disorders. The Druids kindled after their manner two immense fires, with great incantations, close to each other, whilst between those fires the cattle were driven, and if they escaped unharmed it was considered as auspicious as it would be inauspicious for man and beast to be therein harmed, and hence the saying, "Placed between the two fires of Baal." Concerning the mysteries of their religion, the Druids did not commit them to writing, and therefore it is that so little is known of their teachings or of what they taught, and what they did teach is said by some to have been taught in the Greek language, "to the end," writes Sir Edward Coke, "that their discipline might not be made so common amongst the vulgar, nay more, their very names and appellations may serve as a proof of their use of the Greek tongue, they being called Druids from Δρύς, an oak, because, saith Pliny, they frequent the woods where oaks are, and in all their sacrifices they use the leaves of those trees."*

With Druidism departed the forests of the ilex and the quercus from Aran. May we venture to hope that, in the coming changes, Aran may once more be re-afforested, and that the islanders, who have now no coal, no timber, and no turf to burn, may have at least timber to burn in great abundance in the near future?

* II. Coke's Reports, part iii. Preface, p. viii.

The immense fortresses on the islands are said to be the finest specimens of barbaric military structures extant in Europe. Built by the pagan Firbolgs in the first century of the Christian era, these mortarless walls, Cyclopean as they are called, having braved the tempests of nineteen hundred years, still stand. On the large island, and within four miles of our hotel, is Dun Ængus, which, covering many acres, is on a precipice hundreds of feet in height. This fortress, in the form of a horse-shoe, is unapproachable on the sea side, where the Atlantic surges heavily against the solid rock, whose surfaces are seamed, and scarred, and torn by the violence of the billows driven against them by the winter tempests. Unapproachable by an enemy from the sea, it is equally unapproachable by an enemy from the land, the only entrance thereto being by a narrow avenue skirting the edge of the cliff. The fortress consists of three enclosures, the inner, the middle, and the outer. The inner measures 160 feet, on what may be called the axis major from north to south of the horse-shoe on the ground plan, whilst along the cliff it measures 144 feet. The mortarless wall which surrounds this inmost enclosure is about 1100 feet from end to end, by 18 feet in height, and 12 feet in thickness. Now this one wall is made up of three walls, each four feet thick, one against the other, like the coats of an onion, which arrangement occurs in the middle and outside enclosures, and which has this advantage, that if an enemy should succeed in breaking down the exterior envelope, he would find behind it a new face of masonry, instead of the easily disturbed loose interior of a dry stone wall. The space between this inner and the next outside, or middle enclosure, is perfectly clear, leaving ample scope for military manœuvres. The outside wall, which is almost an ellipse, encloses about eleven acres, all studded over with an army of white pointed stones, set slope-wise into the earth, like almonds on a plum-pudding, save where a narrow avenue is left, so that no assailing force could possibly approach the second wall, without having its ranks broken by those intricate piles which answer the *chevaux-de-frise* of modern fortifications. The doorway with sloping jambs of Egyptian pattern through the outer wall admits only one or two assailants together.

Dun Conor, an oval fort on the middle island, is much larger than Dun Ængus, of which we have just been speaking, the axis major of Dun Conor measuring 227 feet. It also stands on a high cliff, and its dry and mortarless walls are built also on the coat of the onion principle.

· Inisheer, the eastern island, contains a circular Dun called Creggan-keel. Furmena Castle, also on this island, was, in later times, the stronghold of the O'Briens—lords of the islands of Aran—and upon these islands are many more fortresses. There is, on the north side of Inishmore, Dun Onaght, a circular Firbolgic fort, measuring 92 feet across; and on the south-west side, *Dubh Cahn*, "the black fort," a Dun or fortress of very rude masonry, of enormous thickness, and overlooking the cliffs.

The Christian remains of the islands are many, and many are the names of the saints still remembered who congregated here in the early days of Irish Christianity. Amongst those remarkable heroes of the Cross, none appears to have been greater than St. Enda, who has left his name everywhere in the islands. To him, indeed, is due much of the success that followed the footsteps of those missionaries who won, in the course of centuries, for Aran the appellation of "Aran of the Saints." Enda was the only son of Conel, King of Oriel, whose territories included the modern counties of Louth, Armagh, and Fermanagh. This Enda had, however, several sisters, the elder being the wife of the King of Cashel, whose death is chronicled in the annals of the Four Masters as of the year 489; the younger was Fancha, the abbess of an abbey, or nunnery, wherein were educated ladies of the court, amongst whom was one remarkable for her great mental and personal attractions. Enda loved her, and hoped that she would one day share with him the glories, such as they were, of the throne of his fathers. His love for his affianced bride amounted to an idolatry, but his idolatry must end, and his idol must die an early death. The abbess brought him weeping into the chamber where the corpse of his loved one was laid. Fancha then reminded him of how favour is deceitful and how beauty is vain, and how the day, dim and remote, would still come when he would be as his affianced bride now was. "Love not the world, nor the things that are in the world!" exclaimed the abbess with a vehemence that her earnestness inspired. That world was then abjured, and straightway he entered a religious order, that of the Regular Canons of St. Augustine, and after years of study and probation, was ordained priest in Rome. He thence returned to the kingdom of Oriel in Ireland, where he built several churches. Having visited his sister and her husband the King of Cashel, the latter was, after much hesitation, persuaded to confer upon God and upon Enda the islands of Aran. Possession of a place so retired and so suited to study and contemplation being thus obtained, Enda introduced there a multitude of holy men, monks to live like the Essenes of old, a contemplative life. He divided the islands into ten parts, and built ten monasteries, each under the rule of its proper superior; whilst he chose a place for his own residence on the eastern coast of the western island of Inishmore, and there erected a monastery, the name and site of which are preserved even to this day in the little village of

Killeany (Kil-Enda), about a mile from Kilronan. Half the island was assigned to this monastery, and multitudes from afar flocked to Aran, which became the home of the learned and the pious. Amongst the remarkable men that there clustered, were St. Kieran, founder of Clonmacnoise, who died in 549, and St. Brendan. The history of the latter abounds with fable, but it is admitted that a thousand years before Christopher Columbus, he crossed the Atlantic and landed on the coast of Florida, where there is a strip of country which, according to Humboldt, in his Cosmos, bore the name of *Irland it Milka*, "Ireland of the white man." The visit of St. Brendan to Aran, previous to his departure to the great western continent, has been described by one of the most musical of our poets—Denis Florence MacCarthy—as follows :—

> " Hearing how blessed Enda lived apart,
>   Amid the sacred caves of Aran-mör,
> And how beneath his eye, spread like a chart,
>   Lay all the isles of that remotest shore;
> And how he had collected in his mind
>   All that was known to the man of the " old sea," *
> I left the hill of miracles behind,
>   And sailed from out the shallow sandy Leigh.

> "Again I sailed and crossed the stormy sound,
>   That lies beneath Binn-Aite's rocky height,
> And there upon the shore, the saint I found
>   Waiting my coming through the tardy night.

---

* The " Old Sea," the ancient name of the Atlantic in Irish.

He led me to his home beside the wave,
  Where with his monks the pious father dwelled,
And to my listening ear he freely gave
  The sacred knowledge that his bosom held.

"When I proclaimed the project that I nursed,
  How it was for this that I his blessing sought,
An irrepressible cry of joy outburst
  From his pure lips, that blessed me for the thought.
He said that he, too, had in visions strayed,
  O'er the untrack'd ocean's billowing foam ;
Bid me have hope, that God would give me aid,
  And bring me safe back to my native home.

"Thus having sought for knowledge and for strength,
  For the unheard-of voyage that I planned,
I left those myriad isles, and turned at length
  Southward my barque, and sought my native land.
There I made all things ready day by day ;
  The wicker boat with ox-skins covered o'er,
Chose the good monks, companions of my way,
  And waited for the wind to leave the shore."

Another of St. Enda's disciples was St. Finnian of Moville—and it was from Aran he set out on his pilgrimage to Rome. Soon after he returned to Ireland, bringing with him a copy of the Gospels, the Papal benediction, and the Canons of St. Finnian. Again departing for Italy, he was made Bishop of Lucca, in Italy, where he died in 588. St. Columba spent years in Aran, and deeply was he grieved at leaving it for Iona. His bitter lament in Irish verse has been translated into English metre by the late Sir Aubrey De Vere, Bart., in part as follows :—

ST. COLUMBA.

1.

" Farewell to Aran isle, farewell !
  I steer for Hy; my heart is sore,
The breakers burst, the billows swell,
  'Twixt Aran's isle and Alba's shore.

2.

" Thus spake the son of God, 'Depart !'
  Oh Aran isle, God's will be done !
By angels thronged this hour thou art :
  I sit within my barque alone.

3.

" Oh Modan, well for thee the while !
  Fair falls thy lot and well art thou,
Thy seat is set in Aran isle,
  Eastward to Alba turns my prow.

4.

" Oh Aran, sun of all the west !
  My heart is thine ! as sweet to close
Our dying eyes in thee as rest
  Where Peter and where Paul repose.

5.

" Oh Aran, sun of all the west,
  My heart its grave hath found ;
He walks in regions of the blest,
  The man that hears thy church bells sound.

6.

" Oh Aran blest—oh Aran blest !
  Accursed the man that loves not thee ;
The dead man cradled in thy breast
  No demon scares him—well is he." *

---

* Sir Aubrey De Vere, " Irish Odes," p. 274.

Amongst the other ecclesiastical notabilities that frequented Aran in the sixth century was St. Fursa, whose life has been written by scores of writers, as well by the Venerable Bede as by Archbishop Usher, the greatest ornament of the Protestant Church in Ireland. The visions of Fursa were, we are informed by the Rev. J. Carey, in his admirable translation of Dante, the groundwork of the *Inferno*. The beautiful imagery of Fursa's fancy, which threw a charm over every subject that he handled, may be well illustrated by his rhapsodies on seeing for the first time the city of Rome, as staff in hand he wended his way to the Eternal City. Falling on his knees, with outstretched arms, he exclaimed, "Rome! oh, Rome! I hail thee, admirable by apostolic triumphs. Rome, decorated by the roses of the martyrs, whitened by the lilies of the confessors, crowned by the palms of the virgins, thou that containest the bones and relics of the saints, may thy authority never fade!"* Strange, is it not, that the first sight of the city of Rome should produce in the minds of men feelings which words almost fail to convey! It was eleven hundred years after Fursa's first salutation to the city of Rome that Edward Gibbon, when musing amid the ruins of the Capitol whilst the barefooted friars were singing vespers in the temple of Jupiter, formed the idea of writing "The Decline and Fall of the Roman Empire," and what his

* Colgani, Acta SS. Hiberniæ.

feelings were on seeing for the first time the holy city he thus in that immortal work informs us: "My temper is not very susceptible of enthusiasm, and the enthusiasm which I do not feel I have ever scorned to affect, but at the distance of twenty-five years, I can neither forget nor express the strong emotions which agitated my mind as I first approached and entered the Eternal City. After a sleepless night I trod with a lofty step the ruins of the Forum." St. Fursa, returning on foot through France, died at Peronne, and his body was conveyed to the island of Aran, where amongst his *quondam* brethren he now, awaiting the resurrection of the just, reposes.

Of the monuments, as well pre-Christian as Christian, in these islands, there are twenty-one, vested in the secretary of the Commissioners of Public Works in Ireland, to be preserved as national monuments. (See next page.)

Ruins everywhere meet the eye of the tourist in Aran—ruined abbeys, ruined monasteries, ruined nunneries, ruined cells, ruined churches, ruined schools, ruined forts, ruined forests, and ruined towers. With one exception the churches of Aran face the east. I heard somewhere, when on the islands, that that is not exactly true, but that they faced the point of the compass at which the sun rose on the day that the foundation stone was laid. Be that as it may, there is the Oratory of St. Banon, which directly faces the

COUNTY OF GALWAY.
BARONY OF ARAN.

Parish.	Townland.	Monuments.
Inisheer, or Lesser Island	Inisheer	Great Fort, with stone-roofed Cells, and O'Brien's Castle. Fort with Mound and Monument. Ruins of Church—Kill-Gobnet, etc. Ruins of Church—Burial-place of Seven Daughters, whose names are unknown. Ruins of Church — Tempúl Coemhan.
Inishmaan, or Middle Island	Carrowntemple Carrownlisheen	Fort Mothar Dún. Fort of Conor. Ruins of Church—Kill Canonagh Ruins of Church—Tempúl Caireach Derquin.
Inishmore, or Great Island	Onaght Killeaney	Fort Dún Ængus. Fort Dún Eochla. Dubh Chathair or the Black Fort. Ruins of Church—Tempúl Benin, with rectangular enclosure and group of Cells. Ruins of Church—Tempúl Brecan and Cross. Ruins of Church—Tempúl beg mac Dara. Ruins of Church—Tempúl more mac Dara. Ruins of Church—Tempúl Assurniadhe. Ruins of Church—Tempúl Ciara Monastir. Ruins of Church—Tempúl à Phoill (the seven churches). Ruins of Church—Tempúl an Cheathrair Aluin. Ruins of Church—Teglach Enda (St. Enda's Church).

north. It is fifteen feet long, by seventeen feet high to the summit of the gables, by eleven feet in breadth. Close by are the remains of the hermitage, partly sunk in the rock, and of some cloghauns, or stone-roofed dwellings. How those solitaries, who for centuries held up the lamp of learning which shone across Europe during the long night which followed the breaking up of the Roman empire, could live in such comfortless cells, it is impossible to apprehend: circular chambers about twenty feet in exterior diameter, with a hole in the stone beehive roof for a chimney, and with an Egyptian-like doorway that a tall man could with difficulty enter. *Teampull-Chiarain* has a beautiful eastern window, with some crosses. Four miles from Kilronan are Kilmurvey and *Teampul McDuach*, a sixth-century church, consisting of nave and choir in beautiful preservation. There are windows there of remote antiquity, with lintels formed of two leaning stones; and there is a semicircular window of great beauty of a more recent date. There is a stone leaning against the eastern gable with a rudely cut opening which seems to have been the head of the more ancient window. The narrow doorway is like the entrance to an Egyptian tomb. Another small church, *Teampul-beg*, together with a holy well and monastic enclosure, is worthy of inspection. At the north-western side of the Inishmore island, and six miles from Kilronan, are the remains of the seven churches, one of which is called *Teampul Brecain*—the church of St. Braccan, who was the founder of the monastery of Ardbraccan, now the cathedral church of the diocese of Meath. The ruined church of *Teampul-saght-Machree* is an object of interest on the middle island. The eastern island in ancient times was called *Aran-Coemhan* in honour of *St. Coemhan* (St. Kevin), brother of St. Kevin of Glendalough. He was one of the most renowned of the saints of Aran, and is believed to have not unfrequently abated storms after being piously invoked. There is a legend in the islands worthy of remembrance by those whose marriages are as yet unblest with children. We speak of that of St. Braccan's bed, where many a fair devotee has prayed and has had her prayers granted, as Anna of old had in the temple of Silo,* when the Lord bestowed on her childless marriage a child who was afterwards the prophet Samuel.

The churches are all of small dimensions—never more than sixty feet in length—at the eastern end of which is not unfrequently a chancel in which the altar was placed. Between the nave of the church and the chancel was the chancel arch of a semicircular form, a very beautiful specimen of which exists in the Protestant cathedral of Tuam. These temples, very imperfectly lighted by small windows splaying inwards,

* 1 Sam. i. 9-17.

do not appear to have ever been glazed. The chancel had usually two or three windows—one of which is always in the centre of the east end, with another in the south wall, another in the south wall of the nave, sometimes, though rarely, two in number. The windows are frequently triangular-headed, but more usually arched semicircularly, whilst the doorway is almost universally covered by a horizontal lintel consisting of a single stone. In all cases the sides of the doorways incline like the doorways in the old Cyclopean buildings, to which they bear a striking resemblance. The smaller churches were usually roofed with stone, whilst the larger ones were roofed with wood covered with thatch. The wells are carefully preserved, the scarcity of water rendering the possession of a well almost as precious to them as to the Eastern shepherds in the days of Rebecca.

The Aran churches, it must be admitted, have little in them to interest the mind or captivate the senses; nevertheless, in their symmetrical simplicity, their dimly lighted naves, in the total absence of everything that could distract attention, there is an expression of fitness for their purpose too often wanting in modern temples of the highest pretensions. The monastic establishments close by contained little that would savour of luxury. The cells of the friars were low, narrow huts, built of the roughest materials, which formed, by the regular distribution of the streets, a large and populous village, enclosing within a common wall a church and hospital, perhaps a library. The austere inmates slept on the ground, on a hard mat or a rough blanket, and the same bundle of palm leaves, served them as a seat by day and a pillow by night. The brethren were supported by their manual labour, and the duty of labour was strenuously recommended as a penance, as an exercise, and as the most laudable means of securing their daily subsistence. "*Laborare est orare*" was a monastic maxim. The garden and the fields which the industry of the monks had rescued from the forest or the morass were cultivated by their ceaseless toil. In the evening they assembled for vocal or mental prayer, and they were awakened by a rustic horn, or by the convent bell in the night, for the public worship of the monastery. Even sleep, the last refuge of the unhappy, was rigorously measured; and it was to lives of self-denial like this that great multitudes in the first century of the Christian era betook themselves. Pliny, who lived when Christ was crucified, surveyed with astonishment the monks of the first century, "a solitary people," he says, "who dwelt amongst the palm trees near the Dead Sea, who increased, and who subsisted without money, who fled from the pleasures of life, and who derived from the disgust and repentance of mankind a perpetual supply of voluntary associates." *

* Pliny, Hist. Nat., v. 15.

On Inisheer island is a signal tower, and near it is an old castle on an eminence. Here is shown the "bed of St. Coemhan," much famed for its miraculous cures. On the south-west point is a lighthouse showing a light one hundred and ten feet in height. It is stated in the *Leabhar-braec* that one of the Popes was interred in the great island of Aran. The same is repeated in one of the volumes of the Ordnance Survey, a work which, never printed, is stowed away on the shelves of the Royal Irish Academy, liable at any moment to be destroyed by a conflagration. In the three or four volumes on the county of Galway are contained, and in the English language, the inquisitions of Elizabeth, the subsequent patents of James I., and much learning touching tithes, fisheries, abbeys, abbey lands, priories, and monasteries, as well as letters on these subjects between Petrie and O'Donovan and other antiquarians employed on that survey.

CHAPTER III.

ISLES OF ARAN, 14TH–18TH CENTURIES.

> " Long thy fair cheek was pale,
>   *Erin Aroon—*
> Too well it spake thy tale,
>   *Erin Aroon—*
> Fondly nursed hopes betrayed,
> Gallant sons lowly laid,
> All anguish there portrayed,
>   *Erin Aroon.*"
>   *Sliabh Cuilinn.*

A.D. 1308. The trade of Galway, which at the time of the Anglo-Norman invasion in the twelfth century was at zero, rapidly rose to a comparatively high figure in the fourteenth century. In 1300 the customs receipts were £24 15s. 2d. at that port, and in 1392, £118 5s. 10d. This augured well for the progressive improvement of the town; but that improvement was blasted for a season by the appearance in the bay of a fleet of pirates who swept the ships from the seas The merchants applied to their powerful neighbour,*

---

* O'Hart's " Landed Gentry," p. 124, edit. 1884.

Dermot More O'Brien, lord of the isles of Aran, to succour them in their straits; and for that succour and the protection which he agreed to give them they agreed to pay him yearly twelve tuns of wine; the trade, commerce, and harbour of the town to be protected, and otherwise by him and his successors defended, from all and every attack of pirates and privateers whatsoever, to which intent and purpose, and for the considerations aforesaid, he covenanted and agreed to maintain a suitable maritime force. This Dermot More O'Brien was descended from Brian [Boru] Boroimhe, slain at the battle of Clontarf in 1014.

A.D. 1334. In this year the islands were plundered by Sir John Darcy, who sailed with fifty-six ships around the Irish coasts.

A.D. 1400. The rebellion of the Mayo and Clanrickarde Burkes in the province of Connaught, consequent on the murder, in 1333, of William De Burgh, Earl of Ulster and fifth Lord of Connaught, caused the overthrow for nearly two hundred years, of the English power in that province. The town of Galway, oscillating in its allegiance between the Crown and the Clanricardes, joined that powerful family against Henry IV., and in their revolt they were joined by the South Isles of Aran. Thereupon the King did by royal license permit certain persons to attack the rebels in the said island, which license is as follows:—

ROYAL LICENSE.

"THE KING to all and singular our admirals mayors and others in our kingdom of England and lordship of Ireland greeting At the supplication of John Roderic William Pound Edward White and Philip Taylor all of Bristol and of Nicholas Kent burgess of Galway in Ireland In as much as our aforesaid liege subjects have given to us security that they shall not nor will presume to make war or afford cause for making war against any of our faithful Irish subjects or attempt anything against the form of the truces entered into between us Wherefore KNOW YE that we have granted and given license and do hereby grant and give licence to them the said John Roderic William Pound Edward White Philip Taylor and Nicholas Kent that they with as many men at arms as they choose to have and provide at their own expenses may take their course for and pass over to our said lordship of Ireland in four ships called by the divers names of 'The Christopher' 'the Trusty' 'the Nicholas' and 'the May of Bristol' and there make war against the rebels and enemies of us in the said town of Galway and also in the islands of Arran which lie full of gallies to ensnare capture and plunder our liege English and further KNOW YE ALL MEN that if said John and William and Edward and Philip and Nicholas shall be able by force and armed power to obtain and take the town and islands aforesaid they may have hold and inhabit the same town and islands taking to their own use and profit all and singular the property of the aforesaid rebels and enemies of us and all that which they shall be able so to obtain and take The right nevertheless and other the rents revenues services and other moneys whatsumever to our royal prerogative there pertaining always saved unto us saving also the right of the son and heir of Roger de Mortimer late Earl of March deceased being within age and within our wardship and the rights of all other liege subjects whomsoever—given at our Palace at Westminster on the 22nd day of May in the first year of our reign—AD 1400 ' By the King himself' "* The town however returning to its allegiance, the above license was in the same year revoked.

A.D. 1485. A monastery was built in this year on the great island for the Franciscans of the strict observance; but this community was doomed to be short lived, for the word had gone forth from Henry VIII. to suppress the monasteries and they were suppressed; and the annalists thus, in the Annals of the Four Masters, A.D. 1537, chronicle not alone their overthrow, but the spread of a new religion in England, "A new heresy and error arose in England through pride, vain-glory, avarice, sensuality, and many strange speculations, so that the people of England went into opposition to the Pope and to

* Pat. Rolls, 1 Hen. IV. 7. m.

Rome. They have demolished the abbeys, sold their roofs and bells, and there is not one single monastery from Aran of the Saints to the '*Straits of Dover*' * that has not been completely destroyed."

A.D. 1560. A tragic occurrence occurred in this year when Teige O'Brien, lord of the isles, was returning, loaded with booty if not with honours, to Aran, from a plundering expedition which he had made into Munster; from one of the seaports of which province he had the rashness with his homeward bound barque to put to sea when a tempest was said by his sailors to be impending. Deceived by the "calm before the storm" he insisted on weighing anchor. It was weighed, and as the starless night was closing and deepening around him, the gale freshened as he advanced—his tempest-tossed vessel struggled amidst the waves, for the wind was high against it— and when the morning rolled the clouds away, a broken spar, an oarless boat, were all that remained to tell the ghastly tale, that every hand on board was lost. At the entrance of the Great Man's Bay, which was far out of their course, is even now shown the spot where on that fatal night they perished.

A.D. 1570. Morchowe O'Brien, in consideration of a sum of money to him in hand paid, conveyed these

---

* "The Straits of Dover" does not occur in the Annals, but the word which does so occur is construed by the commentator to be those "straits."

islands by way of mortgage to James Lynch Fitz Ambrose and his heirs.

A.D. 1575. In June of this year it was agreed between the mortgagor and mortgagee of the islands "that in case the sept of clan Tiege O'Brien, the said mortgagor, should decease and perish, then that James Lynch Fitz Ambrose, the mortgagee, should be their sole heir, and possess, Aran, and all other their lands, and that said O'Brien should not alienate or mortgage any part or parcel of Aran to any person without the mortgagee's consent and license." It appears, however, that Tieg Eturgh, Morchowe Morowe, Conchor McMurchowe, Terrilagh Meeagh, Tieg McTerrilagh, Dermot McMurchowe, Tieg McTerrilagh Oge, and Conchor McMoriertagh, McBrene, gentlemen, all of Aran, and Dermot McCormick McConnor, of the Castle of Trowmore, afterwards on July 14, 1575, appointed Captain Morchowe McTerrilagh O'Brien their attorney for ransoming the isles of Aran from James Lynch, that all such parts as he should so ransom should belong to him (O'Brien) and his heirs for ever.*

It would appear that this Captain Morchowe McTerrilagh O'Brien, of the Clantiege of Aran, on July 14 of the same year, 1575, was in Galway; and being there, was minded to claim the privilege his ancestors had, he alleged, enjoyed of lodgings and meals for two days and two nights in the town, and the "mayor

* Hardiman, "History of Galway," p. 208 note.

calling before him auncient old credibel witnesses, they declared upon their oaths that they never heard of their parents or saw the said sept have no more than two meals in the town, and it was thereupon ordered that said sept shall have no more than two meals, they being always bound to serve attend and wait upon us and in our service as their ancestors had been, and further that it was the O'Brien sept that was bound to give lodging and entertainment to all the commons of Galway, when they shall repair to the islands of Aran. And the said mayor did grant and promise O'Brien to be aiders, helpers, maintainers and assisters, of him against all persons that would lay siege to spoil the islands or castle of Aran or otherwise wrong the said Morchowe or his sept." *

A.D. 1579. Queen Elizabeth, by her charter to the town of Galway, having recited that Richard III., late King of England, out of his abundant grace and for the greater security and safeguard of the town of Galway, willed and ordained that neither MacWilliam Burke, Lord of Clanricarde, nor his heirs, should have any rule or power in the said town of Galway, therein to act, exact, receive, ordain, or dispose of anything without the special license, and by the assent and superintendence of the mayor, bailiffs, and commonalty of the said town of Galway; appointed the

* Hardiman's History of Galway, p. 207.

mayor of Galway to be admiral of her and her successors within the town aforesaid and within and over the islands of Aran and from the said islands to Galway.

A.D. 1580. There died in this year in the islands of Aran an islander who had reached the extreme old age of two hundred and twenty years. This patriarchal inhabitant killed a bullock in his own house every year for one hundred and eighty years.

A.D. 1586. In this year the O'Briens, long the lords of the islands of Aran, "were expulsed from their territory by ye ferocious O'Flaherties of Iar Connaught." The matter was brought under the knowledge of the Crown, who resolved to put an end to the lawless savagery which existed in those parts, whereby one sept could, in times of peace, sail on a plundering expedition against another and expel them, wasting the country with fire and sword all the time; and accordingly a commission, under the great seal, was issued for the purpose of examining the title, if any, of the O'Flaherties to the islands. Having gone through the mockery of an inquisition, the commissioners found that the islands belonged not to the O'Briens, lords of the isles, nor yet to the O'Flaherties, who had no title at all, but that they belonged to her Majesty Queen Elizabeth in right of her crown and dignity; and accordingly she, by her letters patent dated January 15th, A.D. 1587, instead of restoring them to the ancient proprietors, granted them entire to Sir John Rawson, of Athlone, gentleman, and his heirs, on condition that he should retain constantly on the islands twenty foot-soldiers of the English nation.*

A.D. 1588. When the return of the inquisition and subsequent patent granting the lands away from the O'Briens became known, the corporation of Galway thus petitioned the Queen, in favour of Murrough McTurlogh O'Brien : " That the Mac Tieges of Aran, his ancestors, were under her Majesty and her predecessors the temporal captains or lords of the islands of Aran, and held their territories and hereditaments elsewhere under the name of Mac Tiege O'Brien of Aran, time out of man's memory, and that they the said corporation, had seen the said Murrogh McTurlogh authorized by all his sept, as chief of that name, and in possession of the premises as his own lawful inheritance, as more at large doth appear in our books of record, wherein he continued until of late he was, by the usurping power of the O'Flaherties expelled; and we say, moreover, that the sept of the Mac Tiege O'Briens of Aran, since the foundation of this city, were aiding and assisting ourselves and our predecessors against the enemies of your majesty and your predecessors in all times and places, whereunto they were called as true and faithful

* Pat. Rolls, 31 Eliz.

and liege people to the crown of England, to maintain, succour, and assist the town.

"(Signed),   " JOHN BLAKE, Mayor of Galway,
             "WALTER MARTIN, Bailiff,
             "ANTHONY KIRWAN, Bailiff."

Queen Elizabeth heard the appeal, but her Majesty was inexorable. It is more than probable that the O'Briens had caused, at least remotely, the alienation of their inheritance by their own domestic feuds. At the north extremity of Inishmore, the large island, not far from Port Murvey, the islanders show a field where human bones are frequently dug up, and for which reason it is called *Farran-na-Cann*, "the field of the sculls." Here the O'Briens are said at some remote period to have slaughtered each other almost to extermination. This sort of self-destruction is the blackest blot on the page of Irish history. It has always been, and alas! is Ireland's sad and unalienable inheritance. Of the patentee, John Rawson, little is remembered, save that in an instrument enrolled in the Rolls Office, in 1594, he is called " an industrious discoverer of lands for the Queen." The O'Flaherties had now the gratification of seeing the O'Briens, also an Irish sept, turned out of their inheritance, and the same granted to a stranger. After this period the property and inheritance of the islands became and were vested in Sir Roebuck Lynch, of Galway. How Sir Roebuck became proprietor of the islands we have been unable, with certainty, to learn; but we might hazard a plausible guess that Sir John Rawson was granted whatever estate O'Brien had forfeited, and that what O'Brien did forfeit as mortgagor was the equity of redemption in the islands; that consequently Lynch, the mortgagee, remained in possession of the legal estate, and he, on Rawson failing to perform the convenants in mortgage deed contained, foreclosed the mortgage, and thus probably the fee and the equity of redemption became united in one and the same person, Sir Roebuck Lynch.

A.D. 1618. "Indenture of June 20th, between Henry Lynch, son and heir of Roebuck Lynch, of Galway, deceased, of the one part, and William Anderson, of Aran, in said county, of the other, whereby he, the said Henry Lynch, for and in consideration of a sum of £50 of English currency to him paid, did thereby demise and assign all that and those, a moiety of the said three islands to him, the said William Anderson, his executors, administrators, and assigns, for a long term of years, excepting thereout" what must have then been in the islands, "*great trees*, mines, and minerals, and hawks, at an annual rent of £3 Irish, and a proportion of port corn, as therein is set forth."

A.D. 1641. The clan Tiege O'Briens still claimed the islands as their legitimate inheritance, and, taking advantage of the troubles of this troubled year, prepared to attack them with a considerable force, and with the aid of a gentleman of extensive property and influence in the county of Clare, Boetius Clancy the younger. This project, however, was frustrated by the opposition of the Marquis of Clanricarde, then governor of the county of Galway.*

A.D. 1645. The death of Malachy O'Queely, Catholic archbishop of Tuam, occurred in this year. To him John Colgan was indebted for a description of the three islands of Aran and their churches.

A.D. 1651. When the royal authority was fast declining, the Marquis of Clanricarde resolved to fortify these islands, wherein he placed 200 musketeers with officers and a gunner, under the command of Sir Robert Lynch, owner of the islands. The fort of Ardkyn, in the large island, was soon after repaired and furnished with cannon, and by this means held out against the Parliamentary forces near a year after the surrender of Galway. In December, 1650, the Irish, routed in every other quarter, landed here 700 men. On the 9th of the following January, 1300 foot, with a battering piece, were shipped from the Bay of Galway to attack them, and 600 men were marched to Iar Connaught, to be thence sent, if necessary, to the assistance of the assailants. On the 15th the islands surrendered on the following terms:—

* Clanricarde Memoirs, p. 71.

"Articles concluded between Major James Harrisson and Captain William Draper, on behalf of the Commissary-General Reynolds, Commander-in-Chief of the Parliamentary forces in the isles of Aran, and Captain John Blackwall and Captain Brien Kelly, commissioners appointed by Colonel Oliver Synnot, commander of the Fort of Ardkyn, for the surrender of the said Fort.

"(1) It is concluded and agreed that all the officers and soldiers both belonging to sea and land shall have quarters, as also all others the clergyman and other persons within the Fort. (2) That they shall have six weeks for their transportation into Spain or any other place in amity with the State of England, and that hostages shall be given by Colonel Synnot for the punctual performance of these Articles. (3) That Colonel Synnot shall deliver up, with all necessaries of war, by three o'clock this 15th of January, 1652, before which time all officers and soldiers belonging to the said Fort shall march with drums beating to the Church near Ardkyn and there lay down their arms. (4) That Colonel Synnot and the captains, eight in number, shall have liberty to carry their swords, the other officers and soldiers to lay down their arms; that Commissary Reynolds shall nominate four officers of the Fort hostages. (5) That Colonel Synnot, with the rest of the officers and all other persons in the Fort shall, upon delivering their arms and delivering their hostages, be protected from the violence of the soldiery, and with the first conveniency be sent to the county Galway, there to remain for six weeks in quarters, in which time they are to be transported as aforesaid, provided that no person whatsoever belonging to the Fort of Ardkyn found guilty of murder be included in these articles, or have any benefit thereby."

The Parliamentary forces, on taking possession of the fortifications, found several large pieces of cannon, with a considerable quantity of arms and ammunition; they seized also a French shallop with twenty-eight oars and several large boats. The Fort was soon after repaired and strongly reinforced. The late proprietor of the islands, Sir Robert Lynch, was declared a forfeiting traitor, and his right made over to Erasmus Smith, Esq., a London adventurer whose interest was afterwards purchased by Richard Butler, created Earl of Aran in 1662.

A.D. 1653. The castle of Ardkyn was by order of the Lord Protector pulled down, and a strong fort erected in its place. Thenceforth Aran became the place of transportation for the Catholic clergy, whilst on the mainland the most violent acts of oppression and injustice openly took place. The King's arms and every other emblem of royalty were torn down, and fifty priests were shipped for Aran* until they could

* Froude's English in Ireland, vol. i., p. 134.

be transported to the West Indies, they being allowed sixpence a day each for their support.

A.D. 1670. On the 9th of September, Charles II., by patent under the Act of Settlement, granted to Richard, Earl of Aran, the great island, containing 2376 acres statute measure, all situate in the half barony of Aran, county of Galway, at the annual rent of 18$s.$ 5½$d.$ crown rent, payable to the King and his successors. We may observe that the "crown rent" payable to the Crown for lands is the same rent as that which was formerly paid to the abbot or prior of the abbeys and priories confiscated from them under the statute of Henry VIII.—consequently lands held under the religious houses pay crown rent even to this day. Quit rent (*Quietus Redditus*) in the province of Connaught, merely three half-pence an acre, was for the first time imposed at the Restoration, and amounts in the islands of Aran to £14 8$s.$ 4$d.$

A.D. 1687. A grant was made in this year by James II. of three-fourths of the tithes of Aran islands to the Most Reverend John Vesey, D.D., Protestant Lord Archbishop of Tuam, and his successors in the See. One could readily account for his Majesty's bestowing the tithes in question on the Catholic archbishop, but why he bestowed them on the Protestant line appears unaccountable; yet so it is stated in the appendix to the report of the Royal Commission

(1868) on the revenues and condition of the Established Church, page 191.

A.D. 1691. On the surrender of Galway to the arms of William and Mary, a garrison was sent to Aran, and a barrack therein built in which soldiers were for many years stationed.

A.D. 1700. An excursion was made to the islands in this year by one whose name is well known by those who prefer to contemplate the silent life of vegetation to the saddening spectacle of man at variance with his fellow-man. Edward Lnwyd spent many months inspecting the flora of the islands, and having done so, made his report upon them, which is said to be a marvel in its way.

The fee of the islands had become vested in Edmund Fitzpatrick of Galway, Esquire; and he in 1717 demised the whole island of Inisheer to Andrew French of Galway, merchant, for thirty-one years, at the yearly rent of £100, with liberty to cut and carry away as much straw from Straw Island as should be deemed necessary to thatch the houses on the island of Inisheer.

A.D. 1746. The case of *The Mayor of Galway* v. *Digby*, conversant as it was with the royalties of the islands of Aran, caused great excitement in the town during the summer assizes of the year. The action was tried before Mr. Justice Caufield. Mr. Staunton, Mr. French, and another, appeared as counsel for the plaintiff; Mr. John Bodkin and Mr. Morgan for the defendant. The case as stated by the learned counsel for the plaintiff was that from times of remote antiquity the O'Briens were lords of the isles of Aran, or to use somewhat of legal phraseology, were lords of the manor of Aran, and as such, and in their manorial rights they were entitled to all the royal franchises, wrecks, and other strays washed on the shores either of the islands or mainlands of the bay. But the Crown had made a grant of the royal franchises away from the lords of the manor, and had conferred the same on the Admiral of the Bay of Galway, the office of Admiral of the Bay belonging to and being held by the mayor of the town. Now, on the 1st of August, 1745, a great whale, which appeared in the Aran waters, was stranded, and harpooned by the defendant, who obtained from it no less than fifty gallons of oil. The blubber and the whalebone were all there ready to be transported to the Dublin market, and the defendant had actually converted to his own use so much of this royal franchise as would realize a sum of £160. Plaintiff's patent was full, ample, and large; so full, so ample, and so large, that he, counsel, could not but wonder that any lawyer at the bar would sign the pleadings in a case in which a verdict must be directed on the spot for the plaintiff.

Counsel for the defendant did not feel so sure of the success of his learned friend's case as his learned friend did—quite the reverse; he must and at once ask the learned judge for a direction that the verdict be entered for him. He, Mr. Bodkin, admitted that a sturgeon and a whale were royal fish, but they were governed by widely different principles of law. If a sturgeon had been washed on the shore, then the King or his grantee could claim it and grant it to whomsoever they pleased, and the grantee here would not be entitled to it at all; but the whale is not the King's property to grant. Half of the whale is the perquisite of the Queen consort, and that being so, the grant fails. The King is only entitled to the head and the Queen to the tail. It was in old law laid down to be for the Queen's convenience to have abundance of whalebone for her boudoir, and so it is said in Bracton [l. 3. ch. 3], "of the sturgeon let it be noted that the King shall have it entire, but it is otherwise of the whale, for the King shall have the head and the queen the tail, *sturgeone observetur quod rex illum habebit integrum: de Balena vero sufficit si rex habeat caput et regina caudam.*" A verdict was directed against the plaintiff, but whether any after move was made in the matter, or whether the Attorney-General intervened, we have been unable to discover. Suffice it to say that the corporation of Galway interfered no more in the matter.

A.D. 1754. John Digby demised the island of Inisheer to William MacNamara of Doolin, county

Clare, for thirty-one years, at an annual rent of £90.

A.D. 1786. The Catholic archbishop of Tuam, the most Rev. Philip Phillips, D.D., partaking of the hospitality of the parish priest of Aran, stopped a week in the islands: sleeping, however, on a bed of rushes, to which he had been unused, he got an attack of bronchitis, of which he shortly after died at Cloonmore, in the county of Mayo. One would have thought that he could have outlived a discomfort of that trivial kind, for he had been in early life a soldier—not a feather-bed soldier, but a distinguished officer in the Austrian service, and therefore it was that he was called Captain Phillips to the last hour of his life. It is not unworthy of remark that this prelate had, previous to his translation to Tuam, been Bishop of Killala, to which see he had in 1760 [1 Geo. III.] been by James III., King *de jure sed non de facto* of great Britain and Ireland, nominated as appears by the apostolic letter of Clement XIII., dated Rome, November 24, 1760.

In the peerage we find that the earldom of Aran has been twice bestowed on families bearing different names. First in 1662, when Richard Butler (son of James, the twelfth Earl and first Duke of Ormonde) was created Earl of Aran. The honours of this nobleman having expired on his death without issue, the earldom was revived in 1693 in favour of Lord

Charles Butler, brother of James, the second Duke of Ormonde. The story of the second Duke of Ormonde is a sad one. Having filled the highest offices in the state in Ireland under Charles II., he forgot his allegiance to his brother James II., and went over to the ranks of William and Mary. In 1702 he was constituted by Queen Anne Commander-in-chief of the Forces of Great Britain, sent against France and Spain, when he destroyed the French fleet and sunk the Spanish galleons in the harbour of Vigo, for which important services he received the thanks of both houses of Parliament. In 1715 (2 George I.), his grace was attainted by the British but not by the Irish House of Parliament of high treason, and £10,000 set upon his head should he land in Ireland. His grace then retired to Avignon, and died in 1745, a pensioner of the crown of Spain. Upon the duke's death the Earl of Aran became entitled *de jure* to the dukedom, but was not aware of his rights, which he never claimed, being of opinion that the British Parliament destroyed not only the English but the Irish titles of honour of his deceased brother, the second duke. The Earl of Aran died without issue male, December 17, 1758, when the title became and was extinct. After four years, in 1762, the earldom was bestowed on another noble house, that of Gore, in the person of Sir Arthur Gore, and from him is descended Sir Arthur Charles William Fox Gore, fifth Earl of Aran, born on the night of storm, January 6, 1839.

A.D. 1857. The islands were visited by the British Association, under the leadership of Sir William Wilde, M.D., and the results of the visit were subsequently embodied in an interesting pamphlet by Martin Haverty, Esq., long assistant librarian to the Honourable Society of the King's Inns, Dublin. Subsequently the Earl of Dunraven, accompanied by a number of scientific friends, proceeded to the islands, when a series of magnificent photographs were executed, printed, and published under the supervision and direction of the accomplished editor, Miss Stokes, who has edited that ponderous work which throws so much light on the early history of this country.

CHAPTER IV.

*"Where the tints of the earth and the hues of the sky,
In colour though varied, in beauty may vie,
And the purple of ocean is deepest in dye."*
Bride of Abydos.

WE have thus far spoken of the scenery of the islands, and of their natural history, of their antiquities, Pagan and Christian, and of their annals; let us now turn to speak of their people and of what others think of them. Doctor Petrie thus, in 1841, writes:

"I had heard so much of the Aran islanders, of their primitive simplicity, and singular hospitality, that I could not help doubting the truth of a picture so pleasing and romantic, and felt anxious to ascertain by personal observation how far it might be real. Collectively, the inhabitants may be said to exhibit the virtues of the Irish character with as little intermixture of vices as the lot of humanity will permit.

"They are a brave and hardy race, industrious and enterprising, as is sufficiently evidenced, not only by the daily increasing number of their fishing vessels, the barren rocks which they are covering with soil and making productive, but still more by the frequency of their emigration from their beloved homes and friends to a distant country, led solely by the hope that their indefatigable labour may be employed there to the greater ultimate benefit of their families.

"They are simple and innocent, but also thoughtful and intelligent, credulous, and, in matters of faith, what persons of a different creed would call superstitious. Lying and drinking, the vices which Arthur Young considers as appertaining to the Irish character, form at least no part of it in Aran, for happily their common poverty holds out less temptation to the vices of lying and drinking.

"I do not mean to say they are rigidly temperate, or that instances of excess, followed by the usual Irish consequences of broken heads, do not occasionally occur—such could not be expected, when their convivial temperament and dangerous and laborious occupations are remembered. They never swear, and they have a high sense of decency and propriety, honour and justice. In appearance they are healthy, comely, and prepossessing; in their dress (with few exceptions) clean and comfortable; in manner serious yet cheerful, and easily excited to gaiety; frank and familiar in conversation, and to strangers polite and respectful, but at the same time free from servile adulation. They are communicative, but not too loquacious; inquisitive after information, but delicate in seeking it, and grateful for its communication.

"If the inhabitants of the Aran islands could be considered as a fair specimen of the ancient, and present wild Irish, the veriest savages in the globe, as the learned Pinkerton calls them—those whom chance has led to their hospitable shores to admire their simple virtues would be likely to regret that the blessings of civilization had ever been extended to any portion of this very wretched country."*

The devotional expressions of the Aranites and the meekness and resignation with which they bear misfortunes or afflictions is the most striking feature in their character. "I had a beautiful girl for a daughter," said an Aranite peasant, "and I laid her in her grave yesterday, praise be to His holy Name that took her to Himself." A poor woman asking for charity tells you that "she hasn't eaten a bit this day, thanks be to God." Another says, "In troth I have been suffering for a long time from poverty and sickness, glory be to God." Their mode of salutation, too, is worthy of remembrance. The visitor on entering a house says, "God save all here." Meet a man on the road, greet him with a "God save you, sir;" instantly he'll remove his hat and reply, "God save you kindly, your honour." If you pass by men working in a field, always address them with a "God bless the work, boys;" they

* Stokes' "Life of Dr. Petrie," pp. 49, 50.

will answer, "And you too, sir," and if you speak in Irish so much the better, and how their eyes will brighten up at hearing their mother-tongue spoken by "a gentleman's honour!"

To the purity of the morals of the Aran women there are many testimonies. Births of illegitimate children are of rare occurrence indeed. Sir Francis Head, in 1852, made a tour through Ireland, looking into every police barrack as he passed, and when all that was done he published a work entitled "A Fortnight in Ireland." Unsparing in his vilifications of the Catholic clergy, he is compelled to compare the people to whom they minister favourably with those of other countries in the world. Arriving in Galway his first visit was to the police barrack, where he inquired of the officer as to the morals of the Claddagh people, when the south isles of Aran thus came to be mentioned.

"Sir F. Head. How long have you been on duty in Galway?"

The officer replies, "Only six months."

Question. "During that time have you known of many instances of illegitimate children being born in the Claddagh?"

Answer. "Not a single case—not one; and not only have I never known of such a case, but I never heard any person attribute immorality to the fishwomen. I was on duty in the three islands of

Aran, inhabited almost exclusively by fishermen, who also farm potatoes, and I never heard of any one of their women (who are remarkable for their beauty) having had an illegitimate child, nor did I ever hear it attributed to them. Indeed I have been informed by a magistrate who lived in Galway for eight years, and has been on temporary duty in the isles of Aran, that he has never heard there of a case of that nature. These people, however, when required to pay poor-rates, having no native poor of their own in the workhouse, resisted the payment of what they considered a very unjust tax. In fact they closed their doors when the rate was only partially collected."

Three and twenty years after Sir Francis Head wrote the above we read in the writings of Frank Thorpe Porter, Esq., a member of the Irish Bar, long a divisional magistrate for the city of Dublin, and some time acting chief justice for Gibraltar, a further testimony of the worth of the islanders. On his return from Spain, he visited his son, Mr. Frank Porter, M.D., medical officer of the islands,[*] and whilst he was there several cases of typhus fever of a malignant type occurred.

The cottages are, with three or four exceptions, thatched and without any upper storey. The invariable course adopted during the prevalence of the epidemic was to nail up the door of the patient's

[*] "Reminiscences of Frank Thorpe Porter, Esq.," 1875, p. 489.

apartment, to take out the sashes of the window, and render it the sole means of external communication. The medical attendant, priests, and nurse tenders had no other means of ingress and egress, and no objection appears to have ever been made to the system. Doctor Porter was stricken down by the disease, and although ten days had elapsed before a medical gentleman arrived from Galway, the doctor surmounted the fearful malady. "I spent," writes Mr. Porter, "each night in my son's apartment, and during the day he was attended by a nurse. Almost every night I heard some gentle taps outside the vacant window, and on going over to it, I would be told 'My wife is afther making a pitcher of whey for the poor docthor, you'll find it on the windy-stool;' or 'I brought you two jugs of milk to make whey for your son.' When the crisis had passed, and nutriment and stimulants were required, I would be told, 'We biled down two chickens into broth for the docthor, I hope it will sarve him.' Rabbits, chickens, and joints of kid were tendered for his use, and a bottle of 'rale Connemara Puttyeen,' was deposited on the window-stool. The people were all kind and anxious, and when he became able to walk out he was constantly saluted and congratulated; but no person would approach him if they could avoid it. They were all dreadfully apprehensive that he might impart the dreadful contagion. I brought him home as soon as possible, but he and I will always remember most gratefully the unvarying kindness and sympathy we experienced in Aran where they refused to take a farthing either for gratuity or compensation."

On September 3, 1886, Mr. R. F. Mullery, clerk of the Galway Union, thus, in answer to my letter to him, writes:—

"The present poundage-rate, one shilling in the pound, is exceptionally low, owing to a grant of £440, under the 'relief of the distressed Unions Act,' having been made to the islands. The average rate for the last ten years was three shillings in the pound. We never have islanders. There is no hospital, though there ought to be one, on the islands, as the sick poor are deterred from coming thirty miles by boat to the workhouse. The general health is exceptionally good, and very many live to a very old age. I have an opportunity of knowing this, as I have to examine the registry of deaths at the end of each quarter. The islanders as a rule are very intelligent, and quick at picking up anything they can either hear or see; and, best of all, they are a moral people, a case of illegitimacy scarcely ever occurring in the islands, and then it is looked on as a crime of the blackest dye.

"I have the honour, etc.,
"ROBERT F. MULLERY."

The following extract from a letter written by my

learned friend, Philip Lyster, Esq., barrister-at-law, resident magistrate of the district in which Aran is situated, bears testimony to the peaceful and law-abiding character of the islanders :—

"My dear Burke,
                              "Belfast, September 26, 1886.

"My absence from Galway upon special duty in the north has prevented my replying to your note of the 18th inst. until now.

"The Aran islanders as a body are an extremely well-behaved and industrious people. There are sometimes assaults on each other, which invariably arise out of some dispute in connection with the land, and are generally between members of the same family. There are very few cases of drunkenness. I have known two months to elapse without a single case being brought up. I should say that for four years, speaking from memory, I have not sent more than six or seven persons to jail without the option of a fine. There is no jail on the islands. We hardly ever have a case of petty larceny. I remember only one case of potato stealing, when the defendant was sent for trial and punished. There are often cases of alleged stealing of sea-weed in some *bona-fide* dispute as to the ownership, which we then leave to arbitration by mutual consent. I know very little of the history of the islands. In the last century justice used to be administered by one of the O'Flaherty family, the father of the late James O'Flaherty, of Kilmurvy House, Esq., J.P. He was the only magistrate in the islands, but ruled as a king. He issued his summons for 'the first fine day,' and presided at a table in the open air. If any case deserved punishment he would say to the defendant, speaking in Irish, 'I must transport you to Galway jail for a month.' The defendant would beg hard not to be transported to Galway, promising good behaviour in future. If, however, his worship thought the case serious, he would draw his committal warrant, hand it to the defendant, who would, without the intervention of police or any one else, take the warrant, travel at his own expense to Galway, and deliver himself up, warrant in hand, at the county jail. I am afraid things are very much changed since those days. Excuse my not going more fully into the subject-matter of your letter. Duties here are heavy. Believe me,

"Sincerely yours,
"Philip Lyster."

The dress of the islanders is said, by those who understand such things, to be picturesque; but beyond all doubt their shoes, or rather slippers, made of untanned cow-hide with the hairy side out, and without heels and without soles, are the most unpicturesque foot-dress in Europe. These they call Pampoodies. The raw cow-hide, which is cut to fit the foot, is stitched down the instep to the toe and also on the back of the heel. Soft as a glove, the wearer soon acquires an elasticity of step and an erect and noble bearing in his walk, to which the wearer of the more picturesque boot can never attain. There are two things, it is said, not to be found in Aran—corns on the foot and frogs in the fens. The young women on Sundays have their hair trimmed and bound up very tastily; but what ornament can these young people put on equal to the virtuous characters they bear? On Sundays and holy days the churches are well filled, and the altars well served by priests as zealous as the Catholic Church can in Ireland lay claim to—the Rev. Father O'Donohoe, P.P., and the Rev. Father Waters, C.C.

The extreme politeness of the islanders, and their desire to impart any knowledge they possess of antiquarian lore or of the legends or fairy tales with which the islands abound, must strike with force the mind of the observing tourist. Their reverence for the dead, and their affection for their loved and departed friends, impel them to erect, sometimes in long lines on the roadside, square stone pillars about ten feet in height by three feet each side, all of the same measurements, surmounted each with a well-cut stone cross and with inscriptions such as the following: "*Sta viator.* Stay, traveller. O Lord have mercy on the soul of Mac Dara Ternan, who departed this life 26th June, 1842." These monuments of the dead, who are generally interred in far-distant churchyards, have by moonlight a ghastly appearance. The reverence of the Aranite for holy wells is great, nor will he suffer in silence his faith in them to be ridiculed. "Can you," said a stranger, "be so silly as to believe that that well gushing out of the hillside was placed there by a saint, in dim and remote ages?" The peasant replied that a well on a mountain side or on a mountain top appeared to him to be miraculous. "And isn't it, sir, wonderful to see water on the top of a hill? And it must flow up the hill inside before it can flow down the hill outside;" and water flowing up the hill inside or outside was to his mind miraculous. The stranger answered that, "the water may have been forced up from some far-off lake on a higher level." The peasant's answer was, "that may be so and it may not be so, but your honour does not give us any proof that it is so." Wells in all ages and in all places are associated with the marvellous, even from the well of Zem-zem to that on the Aran rocks, and we are not so sure that the geological stranger was quite satisfactory as to his theory of wells on a mountain summit.

Speaking of the wonders by which the native of Aran is surrounded, what wonder can be greater than that of the mirage, an island that is said to rise after sunset from the Atlantic? A phantom island which the people call "O'Brazil, the Isle of the Blest," upon which a city like the New Jerusalem is built, and the old men say that that city hath no need of the sun nor of the moon to shine in it, neither does it need the light of the lamp any more at all. That island with that city has, they say, over and over again appeared far away on the Atlantic. Alison, we remember, somewhere in his charming account of the French in Egypt, gives a note on the mirage of the desert, where the parched-up soldiers of the French republic, in 1798, used to see far-distant lakes into which tumbled the waters of mighty waterfalls. On, on the French soldiers rushed. Alas! the phantom vanished; and so vanishes the phantom city seen on a summer evening from the lofty cliffs of the Aran islands. To follow in search of this "Isle of the Blest" an Aranite peasant once resolved. He had heard of St. Brendan and of Christopher Columbus, and of those mariners who, sailing over the seas in search of fame and of gold, were fortunate enough to find both. The peasant, in spite of all persuasion, set sail. The phantom receded; he followed. Still following, he never returned to Aran again, and his mournful fate is thus sung by Gerald Griffin :—

1.

"On the ocean that hollows the rocks where ye dwell,
A shadowy land has appeared, as they tell;
Men thought it a region of sunshine and rest,
And they called it O'Brazil, the Isle of the Blest.

From year unto year on the ocean's blue rim,
The beautiful spectre showed lovely and dim ;
The golden clouds curtained the deep where it lay,
And it looked like an Eden away—far away.

2.

" A peasant who heard of the wonderful tale,
In the breeze of the Orient loosened his sail ;
From Aran, the holy, he turned to the west,
For though Aran was holy, O'Brazil was blest.
He heard not the voice that called from the shore,
He heard not the rising wind's menacing roar :
Home, kindred, and safety, he left on that day,
And he sped to O'Brazil away—far away.

3.

" Morn rose on the deep, and that shadowy isle,
O'er the faint rim and distant reflected its smile ;
Noon burned on the wave, and that shadowy shore
Seemed lovely, distant, and faint as before.
Lone evening came down on the wanderer's track,
And to Aran again he looked timidly back ;
Oh ! far on the verge of the ocean it lay,
Yet the isle of the blest was away—far away !

4.

" Rash dreamer, return ! oh, ye winds of the main,
Bear him back to his own peaceful Aran again ;
Rash fool ! for a vision of fanciful bliss
To barter thy calm life of labour and peace.
The warning of reason was spoken in vain,
He never revisited Aran again.
Night fell on the deep, amidst tempest and spray,
And he died on the waters away—far away. "

CHAPTER V.

> "Never Boreas' hoary path,
> Never Eurus' poisonous breath,
> Never baleful stellar lights
> Taint *Aran* with untimely blights."
> BURNS.

THE extreme old age to which the inhabitants live in Aran proves the excellence of the air and of the food. Neither asthma, nor gout, nor rheumatism are known in portions of the islands. Formerly there were forests of oak and of pine in Inishmore, which must have been peculiarly suited to those who suffered from diseases of the chest.

The fishery here begins in the spring, and great quantities of spillard, cod, ling, haddock, turbot, gurnet, and mackerel are caught. The natives look much to the herring fishery, which seldom disappoints their expectations. In May the pursuit of the sun-fish gives employment to many, and it appears, from evidence given before the Irish House of Commons in 1762, that sun-fish of average size were worth from £5 to £6 each. Then all manner of shellfish are in abundance in those waters—multivalves, bivalves, and univalves—lobsters, oysters, periwinkles. The Aranite may be said to be an amphibious animal—a fisherman and a farmer, but as a fisherman he is powerless to cope with them whose ships are built for the deep sea fishery. It was as a farmer we had the pleasure of seeing him, and in the court of the Land Commission, which sat in Kilronan on the 20th of July, 1886. The Land Court presented an animated appearance on that day, the islanders crowding in to hear their cases. Unlike any Europeans that we know of, the men sat or squatted on the floor in manner as the Mahometans would in the mosques of Bussorah. Remarkably intelligent, they gave their evidence in court with an ease and precision, especially when examined in Irish, which it was refreshing to hear. Many of the cases stood over from the Land Commission sittings in the islands on June 25, 1885, on which occasion there were ninety-five listed for a hearing, and of these the following, the first heard, is a fair specimen of all the rest, the Commission being composed of Mr. Crean, B.L., Professor Baldwin, and Mr. Barry.

Irish Land Commission.

Michael O'Donel, tenant.

Miss Digby, Landenstown, county Kildare, and the Hon. Thomas Kenelm Digby St. Lawrence (second son of Thomas, twenty-ninth baron, third Earl of

LAND COMMISSION IN ARAN.

Howth—by his second wife, Henrietta Digby, only child of Peter Barfoot, Esq., of Landenstown, county Kildare), landlords.

Mr. Concannon appeared as solicitor for the tenants; Mr. Stephens, solicitor, for the landlords.

Michael O'Donel sworn.

Mr. Concannon. O'Donel, are you tenant of this holding?

I am, your honour.

How long are you tenant?

Since I was born—and that's fifty years ago.

Do you swear that, that you were tenant since you were born? How long are you paying rent?

Since my father's death, about eight years ago last Pathrickmuss,—that's the time I'm the rale tenant. My father and his father were tenants on that holding since the Deluge at all events—couldn't swear longer than that.

Do you swear that?

Well, of coorse I couldn't swear it out and out.

What quantity of land have you in your holding?

Well, twenty-two acres exactly, be the same more or less. [Mr. Stephens, for the landlords, said that twenty-two acres was the true area of his farm.] Five of the twenty-two acres were nothing but rocks and stones, without one blade of grass in them, so that it was seventeen acres of productive land he had, at an annual rental of £3 18s. 6d., and it was not worth that.

To the court. The last change of rent was thirty years ago.

What buildings have you?

The house is my own, and the barn. Both are thatched. [Mr. Stephens did not claim the houses.] Improvements?—Well, there are walls, but did not measure them, and small gardens.

In answer to Mr. Concannon: We claim to be entitled to take the seaweed for manure. We have no turf, nor timber to burn, and have to pay £3 a year for two boat loads of turf. The stock on his farm was a cow and a veal calf, a horse, five sheep, and eight lambs. Shears them every year, but the wool he never sells as he keeps it for his family. As for tillage, he had about eighty stone of potatoes last year, and by his stock he realized £12; that includes £6 7s. 6d. that he received for a couple of veal calves. He had no grain crops. He had a couple of pigs too. As for his stock, maybe it's little he'd have out of them coming home to his wife and childher, and his was a nice wife, thanks be to God. His sheep he brings by boat to the county of Clare, sells them at the fair of Ennistymon. Has to pay freight 3d. a head for sheep and lambs. His cattle and pigs he puts on the mail boat and sails them to Galway—the freight being 2s. 6d. for calves, and a shilling a head for pigs. And wasn't he sixteen days weatherbound in Galway last February, after the fair-day?

Mr. Concannon would produce no valuer, he felt perfect confidence in the commissioners.

This closed the tenant's case.

Mr. Thompson, of Clonskea Castle, county Dublin, sworn. Is the agent on the estate; succeeded his father, who had been agent for many years. Witness has in his custody all the rentals and leases of the estate from 1794. "The rental in 1800 was £2143, as fixed by valuation in that year. In 1812 the rental was £2668; in 1827, £2145 10s. 4d.; in 1846, £1937 17s. 7d.; in 1881, £2067; in 1885, £2067; the acreage of the islands being 11,288 acres. The lands are in the hands of tenants, with the exception of two croggeries which are in my occupation."

The learned chairman, Mr. Crean, B.L., inquired what a croggery meant.

Witness said that "croggery" was a very ancient name for fourths. The entire islands were divided into townlands, which townlands contained 4 or 6 quarters each, every quarter containing 16 croggeries, and every croggery containing 16 acres. Inishmore thus contained 4 townlands and $4 \times 6 \times 16 \times 16 = 6144$ acres. On Inishmaan there are two townlands, which contain 6 quarters each. On Innisheer there is only one townland containing 4 quarters. The tenants have manure and seaweed from the sea shore free of charge. The seaweed was very valuable in 1866, when the kelp made on the islands realized £2577, being £5 a ton. There is no kelp made now, owing to the fall in prices. For twenty years the value of a tenant's interest in a croggery varied from £30 to £90.

This closed the landlord's evidence, and the lay sub-commissioners in due time inspected the farms. The case came on for judgment, and the court reduced the rent from £3 18s. 6d. to £2 7s. 6d., being 39.75 per cent. reduction.

All the other cases were similar to the last.

On Tuesday, July 20, 1886, her Majesty's gunboat was moored at the New Docks, Galway, for the purpose of taking the Land Commission composed of Mr. Crean, Lieut.-Colonel Bayley, Mr. Rice and myself, to Aran. The voyage was one to be remembered. The wind, from the S.S.W., rose to a tempest, not a sail in sight. Nevertheless the vessel held on her course, though the wind was high against her, and she let drop her anchor in due time in the Bay of Kilronan. No mail boat from "Europe" arrived in the islands during the greater part of that week. To fix a fair rent was the object of fifty-four originating notices which now came on for hearing. Of this number two were dismissed on points of law, and forty-nine had their rents fixed, the sum of the old rents being £384, which was now reduced to the new or judicial rent of £231, being a reduction in favour of the tenants of £153, say forty per cent.

This reduction, as a matter of course, was well received by the islanders; but the questions that are irresistibly forced on the mind are, can any reduction of rent improve their condition? And can any tenure of their farms, or any estate therein, however large, raise them from their condition of comparative poverty to that of wealth? And would it be of material benefit to them to sweep from the landlord the last farthing of his rent, and to grant the same to them? And would it not be for their weal rather that they had schools to instruct the young in the natural history of the fish, and in the ways of science connected with the deep sea fisheries, and in navigation and all its kindred branches, such as mathematics, spherical trigonometry, the use of the compass, magnetic needle, the constellations, and nautical tables, etc., together with all the trades incident to fishing such as carpentering, ship building, nail making, sail, net, rope, and line making?

And ought not the young and the old to be familiarized with the name of the Baroness Burdett-Coutts, and with her wonderful works in the cause of the Baltimore Fishery? And would it not be for the weal of the islanders, and of the nation, the Irish nation, that the islanders should be supplied, not for charity, with deep sea fishing appliances, as the Baltimore fishermen have been?

The ignorance of our fishing population is thus

deplored in the report of "the inspectors of the sea and inland fisheries of Ireland," 1887 :—

"It is melancholy to find how deficient our coast population is in all these matters, and that the rising generation are left untaught in arts, from the exercise of which, wealth would be brought into our land, and industry, self-reliance, and temperance inculcated, while the seas around our island teem with fish; so much so that often, when a great capture occurs, quantities of fish are lost from the want of scientific knowledge as to the best means of curing; and, at the same time, Ireland is *importing* about 10,000 tons of cured fish *annually*, when she might be *exporting* double, or even treble that quantity.

"Thousands of pounds are also sent annually from Ireland to England, Scotland, and the Isle of Man, for nets and lines alone, the great bulk, if not all, of which might be kept at home, and our people profitably employed." *

The following letter, from Sir Thomas F. Brady, Inspector of Irish Fisheries, Dublin Castle, on the Aran fishery, is worthy of note:—

"11, Percy Place, Dublin, Dec. 5, 1886.
"MY DEAR BURKE,
"I have your note here. There is a large number of open row boats and curraghs on the three

---

* Report of Inspectors of Irish Fisheries for 1887, p. 10.

islands of Aran, but that is their only mode of fishing; and they can only fish at short distances from the land, and cannot fish except in suitable weather. There is not a single first-class fishing vessel attached to the islands. The people are too poor to provide themselves with such, or obtain security for loans for such. There is one drawback to such vessels being kept, the want of proper harbour accommodation. There is a pier at the north island, but vessels cannot approach it unless near high water, and there is no means of improving it by extension. To make a good harbour it would be necessary to build a new pier into deep water; then, if any quantity of fish is taken, the vessels must lose their time and bring them to Galway, thirty miles. If there were telegraphic communication between the island and mainland, the Galway steamer might be sent out when there was a large quantity of fish, or if there were a number of first-class vessels there, it might pay a steamer to attend them regularly as they do in the North Sea.

"The Manx, Cornish, and French vessels, only go there in the early part of the year when the mackerel sets in. The Frenchmen slightly salt the fish on board, and take them to France and come back again for another cargo.

"Sincerely yours,
"THOMAS F. BRADY."

That a step, however small, in the right direction has been taken, appears from the following letter from Christopher Talbot Redington, Esq., J.P., D.L., of Kilcornan, in the county of Galway :—

"Poor Relief (Ireland) Inquiry Commission,
"Dec. 10, 1886.
"Dear Mr. Burke,
"I have been engaged all the summer, in conjunction with Colonel Fraser and Mr. Mahony, in expending a grant of £20,000 in the scheduled unions under the provisions of the Poor Relief Ireland Act, 1886. We have carried out several works in North and South Aran. The Board of Works are building a pier in the middle island.
"Yours truly,
"C. T. Redington."

The absence of first-class fishing boats accounts for the absence of wealth in the islands. The Aran fisherman sees the French fisherman fishing whilst he becomes a farmer and a labourer at wages not worth working for. The Rev. William Killride, rector of Aran, thus writes :—

"Aran, Dec. 11, 1886.
"Dear Sir,
"Men's wages vary. There is no constant work whatever. Spring and the seaweed gathering for kelp are the chief harvests for the labourer. A labourer

has seldom more than four months' labour in the year; so that it is a necessity on his part to get gardens on hire. Until last year or the year before he got from 1s. to 1s. 6d. in spring, with his diet; at harvest, about 1s. with his diet, three meals in the day, bread and tea for breakfast, etc. When there is a hurry in sea-weeding time he used to get 2s. 6d. and diet, but this lasts only a week twice in the year." The writer then speaks of several other matters connected with the island and about the possibility of growing timber there. "My little grove was planted by myself. I find the greatest difficulty in preserving it, seven trees being destroyed this year. Then I planted every nook and cranny with evergreens; but they were plucked up three several times. I got sick of this thing. Many places in the island were covered with trees. In fact, fifty years ago or so, I have been informed that a large portion of the island grew trees, especially hazel, from 20 to 26 feet in height.

"What kept the poor rate down both last year and this was the amount of relief given out. Mr. Thompson, the agent, laid out £140 on a road, and £136 on seed potatoes. Sir John Barrington has given me upwards of £100 for this object, and this year he gave me £80 or £90 for seed potatoes and £120 for relief and also money to assist emigration and to buy turf. The people will suffer terribly this year for want of fuel. The potato crop is all gone. No fish whatever taken. Any further information you may want I will freely give.

"I am, dear Sir,
"Yours, very sincerely,
"WILLIAM KILLRIDE."

The poverty of the Aran fishermen was equalled until lately by that of the Baltimore fishermen in the south of Ireland. Their altered state of circumstances appears by a report of the inspectors of Irish fisheries on the sea fisheries of Ireland, presented to his Excellency the Lord Lieutenant in the autumn of 1886. The Baltimore fishing boats had been mere curraghs worth about £6 each. Owing to the liberality of Baroness Burdett-Coutts, of imperishable fame, a number of deep sea fishing boats were built at a cost of £600 each, which was lent to the Baltimore men on easy rates of repayment. The report states that at Baltimore, in the year 1885, there were 41,610 boxes of fish caught by fishermen previously unemployed, and these boxes of fish realized a sum of £34,585. Mostly every tradesman in the town was employed; the carpenters in making boxes, the smiths in strapping them round with hoop iron. "Three vessels arrived in Baltimore loaded with ice, and eight hulks were used for storing it, two at a cost of £20 a month, the others were owned by a company of fish buyers, at a cost of £1 5s. a week each. This for ten would amount to £3080, besides a large expenditure on packers." Fancy the like sums scattered in Aran!

At Baltimore in 1886, sixteen steamers were employed in carrying the fish to England, at an estimated cost of £400 each per month.

Over 100 men were employed in the boats used by the buyers; and at a rate of wages which, for twelve weeks, would amount to about £1500, besides a large expenditure upon packers, etc.

In 1886 three vessels arrived with ice, containing 1423 tons, all of which were imported, and eight hulks were used for storing it, owned by a company of fish buyers.

The following instructions to persons applying for loans under the Irish Reproductive Loan Fund, and Sea Fisheries Fund Acts, 37 and 38 Vict. chap. 86; 45 Vict. chap. 16; and 47 and 48 Vict. chap. 21, would be read with delight and acted upon with avidity were it not for the nasty note that appears at the foot of so flaring an advertisement.

"I. Loans will be made as heretofore for the purchase or repairs of boats, vessels, or fishing gear, on the security of borrowers and persons to be joined with them as sureties in a joint and several bond and promissory notes.

"II. In *special cases*, where the Inspectors of Irish

Fisheries shall deem it expedient that a new fishing vessel should be supplied to a borrower instead of money, they may, with the consent of the Lord Lieutenant, recommend loans on the security of the borrowers, and on the security of the fishing vessel to be supplied. In such cases the borrowers must give to the Commissioners of Public Works a joint and several bond or promissory note as the case may be, for the amount of the loan, and also execute a deed providing that the vessel shall be registered in the name of the Commissioners of Public Works, and so continue registered until the loan with interest, and any expense incurred, shall be repaid, and also providing that in default of payment of any of the instalments, by which such loan shall be made repayable, or in default of the borrowers preserving the same in proper order and condition, or in case the said vessel should become in the opinion of the said Commissioners a deficient security for the amount of the loan for the time being unpaid, the said Commissioners may cause such boat or vessel to be sold.

"III. Time for repaying any loan not exceeding ten years.

"IV. Repayment by half yearly instalments with interest at the rate of $2\frac{1}{2}$ per cent. per annum.

"NOTE.—It must be observed that loans under rule No. 2. can only be recommended *under very exceptional circumstances, and to a very limited extent,* as the funds available for loans for new vessels are quite insufficient to meet large demands. It will, therefore, be impossible for the inspectors to do more in carrying out this rule than to recommend loans on the security of vessels in a few cases only, where very exceptional circumstances exist, and only in cases of new first-class fishing vessels being provided for with thoroughly experienced fishermen of good character.

" No loans for the purchase of gear will be made without personal security, as laid down by the rules already in force, see No. 1.

" By order,
" GEORGE COFFEY,
" Secretary.
"Fisheries Office, Dublin Castle, February, 1886."

Of the immensity of the fisheries we can form no estimate. But to the islanders the fisheries are worthless without boats, and without the means of obtaining boats; without funds, and without the means of obtaining funds. Except "under very exceptional circumstances, and to a very limited extent," they are unable to launch out into the deep and let down their nets for a draught. It is said by one party that a different state of things would prevail had the Irish people an Irish Parliament. That may be so and it may not be so; but one thing is certain, that whilst in 1887 no bonus of any kind can be obtained, in 1787 bonuses of many kinds could be obtained, and were obtained. In the 27th year of George III., A.D. 1787, an Irish Act was passed "for the encouragement of the fishery usually called the deep sea fishery." The marginal note of that section, a section too long to repeat, states that "bounties will be given, 80 guineas for the greatest quantity of herrings caught by the crew of any one vessel, and imported between the 1st of June and the 31st of December in any one year; 60 guineas for the next greatest quantity, 40 guineas for the next, and 20 guineas for the next, to be paid on the 1st of January following." By the same Act bounties of four shillings a barrel were authorized to be given for herrings; and by another section, the fourteenth, three shillings and threepence by the hundredweight was allowed for all dried cod, ling, and other fish mentioned therein. Bounties, however, have long since been discouraged by political economists, and loans have long since been discouraged by other economists, and between those scientists money for the improvement of the Aran fishery was never so hard to be got at as at this present time.

From the coastguard return it would appear that the Galway coastguard division is guarded by five coastguard stations, two of them being on the Aran islands, in which there has been an increase in 1886 of two second class and sixteen third class boats solely engaged in fishing. The trawlers work from Barna to the islands of Aran. That trawling injures the supply of fish is insisted upon by the one party and denied by the other. A court of public inquiry was held in Galway, where the entire question was investigated; the result of which investigation will form the subject of a special report. We shall only observe that the Scotch Fishery Board has prohibited trawling in some places in Scotland. "In the Galway Bay trawling was prohibited for a number of years in about half the bay. For about four years it was not followed at all, and, so far as the evidence at public inquiries could be relied on, there was no improvement in the fisheries during the cessation of this mode of fishing in either the whole, or part of the bay. In the case of Dublin Bay trawling has been prohibited for nearly forty-four years; and the question arises whether the fisheries of that bay have increased in that period.

"In other bays no trawling has ever been carried on; and the present state of the fisheries in such places will have to be carefully inquired into." *

* Report of Inspectors of Fisheries, 1887, p. 8.

CHAPTER VI.

*"The darksome pines on yonder rocks reclined
Wave high and murmur to the hollow wind."*

POPE.

HAVING thus far spoken of the wealth that might be realized by the islanders from the waters that surround their islands, let us turn to speak of the wealth that might be realized by the islanders from the islands themselves—wealth produceable neither by patches of potatoes, nor by tillage, nor by minerals, nor by pasturage. On the islands are vast terraces of naked rocks, and there are vast terraces of rocks not naked on which grew those forests of oak, of yew, and of fir of which we have already spoken, when treating of Druidism. To re-afforest the disafforested wilderness has of late occupied the thoughts of the thoughtful in our country. Dr. Lyons, for some time M.P. for the city of Dublin, gave to it much of his attention. He has been taken away, but his mantle has fallen upon another. Dermot O'Conor Donelan, Esq., J.P., of Sylane, near Tuam, teaches us how the people of other countries are enriched by their forests. Having made a tour through the unwooded mountains of Connemara, he subsequently in the present year made a tour through the wooded mountains of the Grand Duchy of Baden. His inquiries and the result of his inquiries in that prosperous country he published in a series of letters in the *Irish Times* and *Freeman's Journal*. To give those letters *in extenso*, however instructive, would fill too many of our over-filled pages, but we may be permitted to make a few quotations from them.

"It is a noteworthy fact," writes Mr. Donelan, "that from the class of lands similar to those that lie waste in Ireland, the recent progress of Germany is generally believed to proceed. Prussia, Bavaria, Saxony, Wurtemburg, Baden, and Alsace-Lorraine have a combined population of 40,644,000. The labour connected with the forests of those countries and their products have been estimated to be worth £9,450,000; and those earnings suffice for the maintenance of about 300,000 families." He then forms a painful contrast between Baden and Ireland—between the German mountain districts, and the mountain districts of the same kind in Ireland where there is a similarity of soil; but there the similarity ends.

"The mountains and bogs of Connemara, with the roots and remains of trees scattered everywhere amongst them, are lying there in their bare and melancholy desolation, and but for the presence of some miserable hovels, the whole scene might be inside the Arctic circle. The mountains of Schwartzwald, however, are covered with forests of silver fir, and by their vast supplies of timber are creating vast industries. In a tour which I made through it some months ago, I observed that almost every branch of wood-work was in active operation, and for miles together the rattle of machinery was hardly ever silent. The manufacture of paper from wood, which is comparatively new, has already assumed very large proportions in South-Western Germany. Second class wood-ends, etc., for paper-making, can be had for about eight shillings a ton; while straw must always cost from 30s. to £2 10s. This difference will gradually transfer the manufacture of paper and papier-maché to this and similar forest districts. Within the last few years several mills have been established for the manufacture of cellulose from wood. They have been found successful, and it is expected that this will soon be among the most important of the forest industries. A list of the objects of which cellulose is the basis would form a curious example of recent invention. In the American Patent Office no less than one hundred and twenty patents have been taken out in connection with cellulose since 1870. Gun-cotton, collodion, celluloid, artificial ivory, handles for knives, etc.; dental plates, cuffs, collars, shoe-tips and in-soles, billiard balls, are a few names taken from a long list, and which will give an idea of the number of trades this one material is establishing in many cities and towns of Germany. Celluloid can be made as hard as ivory or be spread on like paint; it is water proof, air proof, and acid proof. It can be pressed or stamped, planed as wood, turned in a lathe, and it can be transparent or opaque.

"I am not able to state the quantity of basket and wicker-work used in the United Kingdom, but at the lowest computation it must be several millions worth a year, the imports alone being very large.

"It would not be possible to enumerate," he writes, "the number of industries which supplies of timber are capable of developing. Some of those would spring up within twelve or fourteen years, and which are further capable of enormous development. Poplar grows rapidly in Ireland; in twelve years the thinnings are of considerable size, and, according to Mr. Herbert's report on the forestry of Russia (Blue Book, commercial, 31, 1883), it appears that from poplar most of the paper exported from Russia is manufactured. The consumption of paper in the United Kingdom must be over £30,000,000 a year, and if it be probable that mountain forests are likely to be the scene of a considerable portion of its production in the future, what an opportunity is there then of utilizing by means of forestry the waste lands and the cheap labour of Donegal and Connemara. Ever since 1800 the question of the waste lands has been before the public. It was reported on in 1812, and again by the Devon Commission of 1840. Every writer on the industrial resources of Ireland had paid it particular attention. It was mentioned by Sir Richard Griffith, by Munns, by Dutton, and even before 1800 by Arthur Young. There is hardly a Government in Europe which has not undertaken the work of reclaiming and afforesting waste lands."

So writes the author of those interesting letters, and he dissipates an illusion which is prevalent amongst us, namely, that to turn planting into profit requires long years and gross timber. On the contrary, as his observations prove, in their earlier years of growth forests will supply many industries for which old timber is unsuited. A great objection to re-afforesting mountains and rocky districts is the length of time that is generally supposed must elapse before so gigantic a work could become remunerative; but Mr. O'Conor Donelan shows that no great length of time is necessary, and that after a very few years timber would be suitable for the works of which he speaks. Would that the Government would take his words to heart, and do in Ireland what German statesmen have done in Germany! There are men amongst us who would fain believe that Aran is too much exposed to the westerly winds to admit of timber being grown on the islands; but the great roots old in the earth tell of the great trees that grew in Aran many centuries ago.

CHAPTER VII.

SUPERSTITIONS OF THE GROVE.

"Oh the Oak, and the Ash, and the bonnie Ivy tree
Flourish best at hame in the North Countrie."

IN the present chapter we propose to give a few of the legends with which groves were enriched when the worship of the sun (Baal) was the religion of the world—legends yet remembered in Aran. In the groves they offered sacrifices, and "burnt," writes the Prophet Hosea, "incense under the oak and the poplar and the turpentine tree [the pine], because the shadow thereof was good." * And we are told that "Abraham planted a grove in Bersabee, and there called upon the Name of the everlasting God." † The selection of such places originated, no doubt, in the fact that the gloom of the forest was calculated to excite awe, and because they considered that the spirits of the departed hovered over the places where the bodies were buried; and it was common to bury

* Hos. iv. 13.   † Gen. xxi. 33.

the dead under trees, as appears from the eighth verse of the thirty-fifth chapter of the Book of Genesis, where it is stated that when Deborah, the nurse of Rebecca, died, she was buried at the foot of Bethel under an oak tree, and the name of that place was called "The Oak of Weeping;" and when Saul, the first King of Israel, fell at the battle of Gilboe, his bones were buried under an oak tree at Jabesh.* Amongst the Hebrews it was common, before the time of Moses, to plant groves. But the idolatrous nations planted them also; and groves and the places of idol-worship soon became convertible terms. For the purpose, therefore, of extirpating idolatry, the Lord thus spoke through Moses: "Thou shalt plant no grove, nor any tree near the altar of the Lord thy God." † And in after-centuries, when Josias abolished the worship of Baal in Judah, and destroyed them that offered incense to the sun, and the moon, and to the twelve signs, he caused the grove to be burnt there.‡

Whether the groves of Aran were destroyed at the time of the destruction of the religion of Baal and of the introduction of Christianity, or in after-ages, it is impossible now to state. That great trees had existence in the islands in 1618 is certain, as appears by a partly hereinbefore recited indenture of that date, when Henry Lynch did demise a moiety of the three

---

* 1 Chron. x. 12. † Deut. xvi. 21.
‡ 2 Kings xxiii. 5, 6.

islands to William Anderson, his executors, etc., for a long term of years, excepting thereout *great trees*.

The Oak.—The chief object of worship was the oak, which has not inaptly been called "the king of the forest." With its life was bound up the life of a nymph, for the nymphs of trees, called in classics *Hamadryades*, were believed to die together with the trees which had been their abode, and with which they had come into existence. Those that presided over woods in general were called *Dryades*, as the divinities of particular trees were Hamadryades. Not unfrequently has the axe of the woodman been stayed by the voice of the nymph breaking from the groaning oak.

That misfortune was believed to follow in the footsteps of those who wantonly felled an oak is abundantly proved by the soothsayers in the olden time. Often have oaks become attached to the lords of the house with whose existence they were bound for hundreds of years. If the leaves in a living state have prophesied touching the affairs of men, so did the dried timbers, as in the case of the *Argo*, when they warned the Argonauts of the misfortunes that awaited them. Not unfrequently has the falling of a branch of the oak tree warned the protecting family of coming disasters. The idols in idolatrous times were manufactured from its wood, though more frequently from that of the ash, and from it was cut the yule-log which served to maintain the perpetual fire. Once a year all fires and lights but one were extinguished, and that was the oaken log, from which every other fire in the islands was with much ceremony relighted.

The medicinal qualities of the tree, and the charmed life it bore, prophetic, as we have said, and causing diseases to depart by its spells and incantations, must have made its existence, if it knew anything at all about it, a happy one. The Irish of the "oak" is *Dará*, and many an Aranite bears that name.

Now, there was a blessed Saint, "Mac Dara," who lived in those islands long ages ago, and there was a renowned statue of him made of oak, which the people venerated with an idolatrous veneration. It was in vain that the Catholic clergy called on them to desist from kneeling before the graven image, and from swearing on it rather than on the Book of the Gospels, on which all men swore. Malachy O'Queely, Roman Catholic Archbishop of Tuam, was, however, resolved to put down an exhibition which he considered a scandal to the Catholic Church, and so, coming to the islands in 1645, he tore down the statue and flung it into the sea; but ill luck awaited him. In the same year he was sent by the Supreme Council of Kilkenny to accompany the confederate troops to Sligo, which had been lately taken by the Parliamentary forces. He did so, and the warrior archbishop rushed to the relief of the town, and for a season dislodged the enemy; but the tide of victory turned, the Irish were routed, and the body of the prelate was literally cut to pieces. Upon him was found that treaty with Charles I. which afterwards helped to bring the unhappy king to the scaffold.

Another of the superstitions that attaches to the king of the forest is that, if his majesty leafs before the ash, the coming season will be dry; if, however, the ash leafs before the oak, then the coming season will be wet.

> "If the oak's before the ash,
> Then you'll only get a splash;
> If the ash precedes the oak,
> Then you may expect a soak."

Of the Irish oak and of the horror that insects have of that tree, we may form an estimate from Hall, who, in his Chronicles, says that "William Rufus builded Westminster Hall, and the oaks with which the said Hall was roof'd were felled in Oxmanstown Green, near Dublin, and no spider webbeth and breedeth in that roof of oak even to this day." Of the remote pedigree of the oak we need not speak further than to remind those who are curious about such matters that the oak all over the world is said to be the first created of all trees, and next to it comes the ash.

The *Ash* is "the Venus of the forest." On ashen sticks (dreadful in matters of witchcraft, as appears from the evidence given in the case of "the Dame Alice Kettler," tried for witchcraft in Kilkenny, in 1324) witches were wont at night to ride "through the fog and filthy air." To love-sick maidens the even ash leaf—that is, where the leaflets of the leaf are even in number—is of priceless value, "and note that if a youngster meeteth and plucketh an even ash leaffe and a four leaffed clover [shamrock], they are most certaine to meet their husband or wyfe, as the case may be, before the day passeth over;" and so runs the old saw—

> "And if you find
> An even-leaved ash and a four-leaved clover,
> You'll see your true love 'fore the day is over."

Strange that the mountain ash, the *rowan tree*, should be held in horror by witches. "Of it whip-handles are made, for the bewitched and stumbling horses thereby become unbewitched and unstumblers." So also the housewife should, before turning the cows out to grass for the summer, tie a switch of mountain ash with a red worsted thread around the cow's tail. The churn, so often bewitched of its butter, is certain to withstand the evil eye when the churn-staff is manufactured of the rowan tree. The roots of the ash or the mountain ash, in Aran, are of rare occurrence; we shall, therefore, pass on to the *aspen*, of which it is said that it alone refused to bow, as the other trees did, to the Redeemer, and that for such conduct the aspen leaf all over the world trembleth even to this hour.

The Elder.—The most unlucky of all trees is the elder, now a mere bush; for out of it was made the cross of Christ, and from one of its boughs Judas hanged himself. In Scotland this tree is known as the bourtree, and hence the rhyme—

> "Bourtree, bourtree, crooked wrung,
> Never straight and never strong;
> Ever bush and never tree,
> Since our Lord was nailed to thee."

The mushrooms growing in or near the elder are known as Judas's ears, of wondrous virtue in curing coughs.

> "For a cough take Judas' ear,
> With the parings of the pear;
> And drink this without fear."

The superstitions attached to this tree are many, and to tell them would fill a volume.

Stumps of *Pine* and *Fir* are numerous in the Aran islands. The fir tree has been ever highly esteemed. It was amongst the materials employed in the building of Solomon's temple. Together with the pine it was held in such veneration in France, that St. Martin met with the strongest possible opposition when he proposed the destruction of the holy fir groves. The fir grew luxuriantly in Palestine; and the Prophet Hosea saith that the Lord will make Ephraim flourish " like a green fir tree."* And another prophet, Ezechiel, informs us, in the fifth verse of the twenty-seventh chapter of his prophecy, that the navy of Tyre was constructed of this tree, whilst the masts were from the cedars (pines) of Libanus. It was the timber, too, used for the manufacture of musical instruments in Israel; for in the Second Book of Samuel (ch. vi. 5) it is written that "David and all the house of Israel played before the Lord on all manner of instruments made of *fir wood*, even on harps, and lutes, and timbrels, and cornets, and cymbals." And when Hiram, King of Tyre, sent timber to Solomon for the building of the temple, it was the cedar and the fir † he sent, for which he was allowed twenty thousand measures of wheat. It was, in Palestine, a tall tree, on the tops of which, we are informed somewhere in the Psalms, the storks built their nests.

The *Holly*, or *Holy*, and the *Ivy* are indigenous in the soil of Aran. In idolatrous times holly was planted, according to Pliny, in the neighbourhood of dwelling-houses, to keep away spirits and all manner of enchantments. There can be no doubt that those who believe dreams to be other than the wanderings of the fancy can on any night have steady sensible dreams of a reliable nature if they bring home in their handkerchief (observing the strictest silence all the time) nine leaves of thornless holly and place the same

* Hos. xiv. 9. † 1 Kings v. 10, 11.

under their pillow. Amongst the conversions of the trees of the forest from the pagan to the Christian faith, that of the ivy was the most remarkable; it no longer adorns the brow of a drunken Bacchus, but is now entwined in wreaths over the altar at the midnight Mass on Christmas night. Nevertheless, they that would look into futurity can still read in the ivy leaf of what is coming to pass in after-times. Place a leaf, on New Year's Eve, in a basin of water, and take it out on the eve of Twelfth Night; if it come out fresh, health is on the house; but if it come out spotted, sickness and death are sure to follow.

The *Hawthorn* and *Blackthorn* grow freely in the islands. Need it be told that the antipathy between these shrubs is so great that the one is never found to be growing naturally near the other? Of course, if planted together, they will struggle on for a time; but one or other generally sickens and dies; for there is a controversy between them as to which had the misfortune to supply the crown of thorns to Christ on the night of the Passion. The peasantry in England, Scotland, and France believe it was the hawthorn, and they look on it as an outrage to bring in flowering hawthorn in May to their houses, it being unlucky and accursed ever since that dreadful night preceding the Crucifixion. So also the blackthorn in Austria and the south of Europe is considered unlucky; as it is there insisted on that *it* supplied the thorns, wherefore it is doomed to blossom when no other tree of the forest dares, in the teeth of the poisonous Eurus, so to do. On which side the truth lies we shall not venture to speculate; but our astonishment is great when we learn that the walking-stick of Joseph of Arimathæa was of hawthorn, that in Glastonbury he stuck it accidentally in the ground, and that ever since it and its descendants bud, blossom, and fade on Christmas Day!

The Rose.—" I am the Rose of Sharon." In the East it is the pride of flowers for fragrance and elegance. It was used amongst the ancients in crowns and chaplets at festive meetings and religious sacrifices. A traveller in Persia describes two rose trees fully fourteen feet high, laden with thousands of flowers, and of a bloom and delicacy of scent that imbued the whole atmosphere with the most exquisite perfume. Originally it was white, and the white moss-rose was suspended over the door of the Temple of Silence; whence it is that secrets are said to be told "under the rose." At convivial banquets in Greece the guests not unfrequently wore chaplets of roses, and anything said by them whilst wearing the emblem of silence was not to be repeated. The white rose was the emblem of purity, and the term "Mystical Rose" is applied by the Catholic Church to the Virgin Mary. Under the cross there grew, amongst the wild flowers of Calvary, a multitude of white roses, some of which were reddened with the blood of Christ. From these comes the red rose, emblematic, not alone of purity, but of martyrdom. The tomb of the Virgin (the Rose that never fades) was found by the apostles to be filled with roses after the Assumption. Her altars ever after have been decorated with roses, and it was a high privilege in the Middle Ages to have a garden where no other flower was admitted. These gardens, called rosaries, may have suggested to St. Dominic the name given to that collection of prayers which he arranged, and which he called the Rosary.

The love of the nightingale for this flower is proverbial in the East. It is unnecessary, of course, for us to remind our readers that the white and red roses were the badges of the rival houses of York and Lancaster.

As for the elm and the beech, countless superstitions are attached to these trees, but as we fail to find that they existed in Aran, so we shall not prosecute further our inquiries on this head.

Ferns.—Not the least interesting amongst the botanical curiosities of Aran are the ferns, that carry their seed on their backs—a seed that has, it is said, the extraordinary property of making the person in whose shoes it is placed instantly invisible to all but himself. So Shakespeare has it, too, in his play of "1 Henry IV.," act ii. scene 1:

"We have the receipt of fern seed, we walk invisible."

A painful illustration of this property occurred, it is told, when once upon a time a man was looking for a foal that had strayed from his stable. He happened to pass through a meadow just as the fern was ripened, some of the seeds of which were shaken into his shoes. After a wearisome and fruitless search during the night he returned all travel-soiled in the morning, and sat down in his house to join the family at breakfast. He was amazed to see that neither wife nor children welcomed him home, nor showed the slightest concern at the night he had spent, nor even inquired about the result of his search. At length, breaking silence, he said, " I haven't found the foal." All were startled, and they looked everywhere to see where he was hiding. Believing that his family were treating him with contempt, he repeated, in a towering passion, "I have not found the foal!" They all sprang to their feet, and his wife called him by name to give over that nonsense, and to come out from his hiding-place. The creaking of his shoes was distinctly heard, though the wearer thereof could not be seen. At length, in a voice of anger, he repeated, as he planted himself opposite his wife at the foot of the table, "I say, I have not found the foal!" Need we tell the terrors of the family? But just then he remembered that he had, on the previous night, crossed a meadow loaded with ferns, and that some of the seed might have got into his shoes, and that he was therefore invisible.

Flinging them off, he at once became visible to everybody.

Fern seed has also the valuable property of doubling a man's power in the working field, several examples of which are given by writers on this interesting subject.

The *Fairy Flax* of Aran we have frequently spoken of in the preceding pages, and that flax may be spun from year's end to year's end, and little realized thereby, unless, indeed, "the good people," as the fairies are called,* take the spinner under their protection. Now, there was once a man in humble circumstances, who had an only daughter, the most beautiful creature that ever was seen. She spent much of her time spinning, but to no purpose. At length a hideous dwarf, lame and blind of an eye, came to her one day as she was spinning, and presented her with a distaff full of flax, upon which, he said, there was enough for her whole life, if she lived a hundred years, provided she did not spin it quite off. On she went spinning, but never spinning to the end, and her loom produced the choicest of stuffs, for which

---

* Numbers of books treat of the superstitious belief in fairies. The Irish fancy that they are the "fallen angels" mentioned in Jude 6, and that on the day of judgment they will be released from their hapless condition (2 Peter ii. 4). The belief in fairies is universal in Mahomedan countries.—*Vide* "Lalla-Rookh," "Paradise and the Peri."

she received prices almost fabulous! Day by day her wealth increased, and after a time she felt assured that the produce of her labour had now secured so sure a market that it made little difference whether she spun the fairy flax right off or not; so, to try what would be the effect, in her curiosity she spun it to the end. In a moment the wheel stopped, and she had ever after to repent the curiosity that stripped her of immense wealth.

The spinning-wheel in Aran, the old crones say, should never spin on Saturday. Whence this keeping holy the Saturday I know not; but it does look as if they who kept the Saturday holy, were of Israelitish descent—were, perhaps, of the lost tribes carried into Nineveh at the time of the Captivity by Salamanassar, 730 B.C.!* Now, there were two old women indefatigable spinners, whose wheels never stood still, though they were by the wise men warned not to spin on Saturdays. At length one of them died, and on the Saturday night following she appeared to the other, who was as usual busy at the wheel, and showed her her burning hand, saying—

"See what in hell at last I've won,
Because on Saturdays I've spun."

Hemp.—I don't remember seeing hemp growing in Aran to any great extent. Sowing the seed of hemp

* 2 Kings xvii. 6.

on All Hallows' Eve in some parts of the country, and on St. John's Night in others, is described in the following lines from Gay's "Pastorals":—

> "At eve last midsummer no sleep I sought,
> But to the field a bag of hemp seed brought:
> I scattered round the seed on every side,
> And three times in a trembling accent cried,
> 'This hemp seed with my virgin hand I sow,
> Who shall my true love be the crop shall mow.'
> I straight looked back, and, if my eyes speak truth,
> With his keen scythe behind me came the youth.
> 'With my sharp heel I three times mark the ground,
> And turn me thrice around, around, around!'"

The *Hazel*, one of Thor's trees, is generally used as a divining-rod to discover mines and lost treasures supposed to be hidden underground. The person who seeks for the treasure takes a hazel rod with an end in each hand, and then slowly walks over the ground, keeping the rod in a horizontal position before him; when passing over the spot it bends down like a bow in the middle, towards the place as if it were magnetized, as the needle turns to the pole. Beyond a doubt the hazel is known to miners, and to those who look for minerals underground, as the divining-rod.

And now, bringing our legends to a close, we shall bid farewell to these lonely and lovely isles, and in bidding them farewell we shall merely ask how it is that the travelling English public travel not into these islands, where frosts never wither, where snows never rest? And so farewell to Inishmore, the island-home of St. Enda—Inishmore—once

> "Notissima famâ
> Insula dives opum, *Hiberniæ* dum regna manebant
> Nunc tantum sinus, et statio mala fida carinis."

APPENDIX A.

"Adorned with honours on their native shore,
Silent they sleep and dream of wars no more."
POPE'S *Iliad*.

WE have spoken so much in the foregoing pages of the O'Briens, lords of Aran, that we feel inclined to say a word as to, who those O'Briens were, whence they came, and whither they went; and first, let us state that their pedigree is traced by Irish genealogists to a date earlier than the Christian era. The O'Briens, lords of Aran, were descended from Bryan Boroimhe, King of Thomond and monarch of all Ireland, who conquered and fell at the battle of Clontarf on April 23, 1014, when the Danish power, all over Ireland, was scattered to the four winds of heaven. In the third generation after the death of Bryan, his descendant Dermod sat on the throne of Thomond, and this Dermod had sons and daughters, and the eldest of the sons was called Turlough, who in 1118 became, on his father's death, King of Thomond, whilst his younger brother was Mahon, and his youngest brother was Teige; and the clan MacTeige for 470 years ruled those islands, we have no doubt, with a very equitable and a very paternal rule, and wholly unhampered with legislative bodies such as a Witenagemot, or with the parliamentary institutions of the Normans, where the members then, as now, had the liberty of speaking, sometimes very plainly, their minds—as, indeed, the Norman name of our legislative assembly imports: *parler-les-mens*, a place for "speaking their minds." That the Corporation of Galway recognized the power of the O'Briens, lords of the isles, is plainly told in the foregoing pages, where we remember that twelve tuns of wine were annually paid to the lord for sweeping the sea, as it were with a broom, clean of the Algerine pirates that then infested the high seas; and there can be little if any doubt that the O'Briens were ready, from time to time and at all times, to massacre the foe wherever they met him, and to convert his ships to their own use and behoof in manner and form as by their indenture of treaty was provided. It is not for us to criticize with critical pen the policy of the respected lord of the isles, who, in 1560, was swallowed up in the deep, near the Great Man's Bay, when he was returning from Thomond loaded with the booty which, at the point of the sword, he had won from the subjects of his cousin O'Brien of Thomond; for it does not appear that ties of blood preserved his Majesty of Thomond from the vengeance of his lordship the lord of the isles, or, *mutatis mutandis*, the lord of the isles from the vengeance of his Majesty. "An eye for an eye and a tooth for a tooth," was their maxim, and it may have been good law where the antagonists had each two eyes and two teeth; but the vengeance was dreadful when the punished party had only one eye and one tooth. He was then blinded and untoothed out and out; and frequently such dreadful vengeance did await the conquered. Let us not, however, be too hard on the conquerors when we remember that David sawed his prisoners in two, and drove harrows over them in a harrowed field.* The O'Flaherties, an equally warlike race, dispossessed the lords of the isles, and in 1588, the very year of the Spanish Armada, Queen Elizabeth finally confiscated their territories, and now the name of O'Brien is forgotten in Aran. Not so on the mainland; the O'Briens are still in Thomond and elsewhere, as, it is to be hoped, they will be for centuries yet to come. The lords of the Isles of Aran are extinct. The last of the male line was John O'Brien of Moyvanine and Clounties, whose daughter Sarah was married to Stephen Roche, from whom is descended the present Thomas Redington Roche, of Ryehill, Esq., J.P., Co. Galway. Amongst the families or this house still existing in Thomond, are the noble house of Inchiquin and the O'Briens of Ballynalacken, both of whom trace up, in an unbroken succession, to Bryan Boroimhe, who, like Leonidas at Thermopylæ, fell fighting the foreign foe for the liberties of his country.

The title of Inchiquin dates from the year 1543, but no title was required to ennoble those who were of the blood of kings, and were "nobler than the royalty that first ennobled them." The untitled aristocracy in England are often superior to the titled aristocracy, who cannot trace back farther than the Wars of the Roses. Now, the last King of Thomond resigned his royalty to Henry VIII., who in return, by patent A.D. 1543, bestowed upon Murrough O'Brien, and upon the heirs male of his body, the title of Baron of Inchiquin. This Murrough had two sons, the elder Dermot, and the younger Donough, and Dermot on his father's death became Baron of Inchiquin; and so the title descended from father to son until the year 1855, when James, the twelfth baron, who was also seventh Earl of Inchiquin (creation A.D. 1654) and third Marquis of Thomond (A.D. 1800), died without issue

* 2 Sam. xii. 31.

male, when the earldom and marquisate expired. Thereupon the father of the present baron, who was also a baronet, and brother to William Smith O'Brien, celebrated as Member of Parliament and leader of the Irish people, knowing his descent from Donough, second son of the first baron, instructed his counsel to bring his case before the Committee of Privileges of the House of Lords, to whose satisfaction he proved that he was heir male of the body of the first baron, and thereupon he was confirmed in said barony, and became thirteenth baron.

Let us now go back to Dermod, the third generation from Bryan Boroimhe, which Dermod died, as we said, in 1118, leaving three sons, the eldest Turlough, King of Thomond, the younger Mahon, and the youngest Teige, lord of the isles; from Mahon is sprung Marshal MacMahon, whose acts and deeds are known of by all men.

This Turlough, King of Thomond, was ancestor of Teige O'Brien, who married Annabella, daughter of Ulick McWilliam Burke, of Clanrickarde, known as "Ulick of the Wine," and by her had, with other sons, Turlough Don, King of Thomond in 1498, and Donal. Turlough Don was ancestor of the family of Inchiquin, of which we have spoken, and from Donal sprang Turlough O'Brien, who was married to a grandniece of Sir Toby Butler, better known as the jovial Sir Toby, the great luminary of the Connaught Circuit, Solicitor-General for Ireland under James II., and the celebrated lawyer who drafted that treaty which will be remembered by all generations as the broken Treaty of Limerick. Turlough was the grandfather of John O'Brien, of Ballynalacken, who died in 1855, and of James O'Brien, Esq., Q.C., who was Member of Parliament for the city of Limerick from 1854 to 1858, when he was raised to a judgeship in the Queen's Bench. It is too near our own time to speak of that learned lawyer further than to say that "he judged not according to appearance, but judged just judgment;" that in him the prisoner at the bar found a merciful judge, and at the same time one who held the scales so that crime could not escape with impunity. Let us hope that when he went to a higher court he reaped the rewards promised to a just judge; and let us hope that those who come after him of his name and race may, when their turn comes, follow in his footsteps, and thus show that the wisdom of the wise still dwells in the brehons of the Celtic race.

The Ballynalacken O'Briens are now represented amogst the landed gentry by James O'Brien, J.P., D.L., and they are also represented at the Bar by his brother, my learned friend, Peter, late Sergeant O'Brien, now Solicitor-General for Ireland.

APPENDIX B.

STATISTICS OF ISLANDS OF ARAN.

Area, 11,288 acres.
Population—Census 1815, 2400
„   „   1871, 3049; increase, 640
„   „   1881, 3163   „   114
Inhabited houses, 1815   395
„   „   1881   576   „   181
Petty Sessions District, Aran.

Religion of Aranites, 1871, 2993 Roman Catholics
„   „   „   55 Protestant Episcopalians
„   „   „   1 Presbyterian
                        ―――
                  Total 3049

Religion of Aranites, 1881, 3118 Roman Catholics; increase, 125
„   „   „   44 Protestant Episcopalians; decrease, 11
„   „   „   1 Presbyterian
                        ―――
                  Total 3163

Number speaking Irish only in Aran, 1871 ... 835
„   „   English and Irish   „   ... 1924
„   „   Irish only, 1881   889
„   „   English and Irish, 1881 ... 1829

STATISTICS OF ARAN.

Constabulary barracks, 1871	1
,, ,, 1881	3
Number of constabulary, 1871	6
,, ,, 1881	18
Coastguard barracks, 1881	2

Quarter Sessions—Galway.
Petty Sessions—Held on the islands.

Roman Catholic churches in Aran	4
Protestant Episcopal church	1
Protestant church accommodation	180
Annual income of parish priest, 1801	£60*
,, ,, Protestant incumbent	£125†
National schools in islands	4
Average attendance, Sept., 1886, to June, 1887	524

Manager, Rev. M. O'Donoghoe, P.P.

Fishing boats on islands, 1st class, 1887	0
,, ,, 2nd ,, ,,	34
,, ,, 3rd ,, ,,	130
Poor-law valuation	£1576
Rent, 1881	£2067
Average poor rate, last ten years	3s. in the £
Paupers in workhouse	0
Distance of workhouse from islands	30 miles
Numbers receiving outdoor relief	43
Grand jury works on island, Spring assizes, 1887	0
Grand jury cess ,, ,, ,,	£34 12s. 2d.

* Vide return made in 1801 by Most Rev. Edward Dillon, D.D., Roman Catholic Archbishop of Tuam (Lord Castlereagh's Correspondence, vol. iv. p. 126). I can find no subsequent return.

† Charles's "Irish Church Directory."

Crown rent (*sup*, p. 45)	18s. 5½d.
Quit rent (*sup.*, p. 45)	£14 8s. 4d.
Labourer's wages	1s. *per diem*
,, ,, spring and harvest	1s. 6d., with diet

THE END.

PRINTED BY WILLIAM CLOWES AND SONS, LIMITED,
LONDON AND BECCLES.

www.ingramcontent.com/pod-product-compliance
Lightning Source LLC
Chambersburg PA
CBHW031354160426
43196CB00007B/809